THE GReeTiNG CARd WRiTeR'S HANDboOK

EdiTeD bY
H. Joseph CHAdwick

Writer's Digest—Funk & Wagnalls
380 Madison Avenue, New York, New York 10017

For
Beverlee
My playmate . . . who makes it all worthwhile.

Kimberlee, Hollee, Steve, and Barbara
My delights . . . who make it all necessary.

Harold T. Chadwick
My father . . . who taught me that it doesn't make any difference how many times you get knocked down, as long as you keep getting back up.

Barbara Brewer
My mother-in-law . . . who is all things nice.

Preface

If you're looking for a "fun thing" to do between working in your garden and bowling on Wednesday nights, if you're looking for a hobby because you've got some extra time on your hands ("Something that doesn't take too much effort."), if you need extra money and want something you can "dash off" in the evenings after your serious job, then don't waste your money buying this book. It's not for you!

BUT . . . if you seriously want to learn how to write greeting cards, if you are willing to spend the time, blood, sweat, and tears it takes to learn the craft of writing greeting cards, if you really and seriously want to become a professional in this great, exciting, wonderful — and add to that fun and sometimes even hilarious — business of writing and selling greeting cards, then this book is for you, and you are for us! Why?

Because each and every one of us in this book is a hard working, no nonsense professional greeting card editor or writer. We make our living, or a darn good portion of it, in this business, and we resent anyone who approaches it as a "fun thing," or something they can do as a "hobby," or on a Sunday afternoon after "tea" or "golf" — that is, if they can find the time. So if you're the kind of person who believes that writing, even humor writing, is a serious business, who is willing and eager to devote all the energies needed to learn how to become a professional in this business, then *you* are the person we wrote this book for!

There are no "secrets" in this book, no "shortcuts," no "ideas from out of the sky" nonsense, no "see how easy it all is and my what fun we are having!" type of thing. What this book does have in it are good, practical, proven methods and techniques for writing greeting cards — any kind of greeting card: conventional, informal, inspirational, humorous, studio, and juvenile. Also mottos, buttons, and humorous stationery.

On top of that, the book shows you how to write when you want to write. Not just when the muse or mood, or whatever fancy name you give it, strikes you, but any time of the day or night!

The book also shows you how to write funny ideas, cards with attachments, mechanical cards, what to write about, how to set up records, code your ideas, how to submit, what editors like and don't like; it has a bibliography of *useful* books and magazines (and *believe* this bibliography, Friend, it's not just for appearance . . . . we put in it *only* the books that we personally are using to help us write greeting cards!), a renewable market list, a glossary of greeting card terms, and an index to help you locate information in a hurry when you need it.

It's also loaded with hundreds of examples of good greeting cards for you to use as models and to help key off fresh ideas of your own.

In short, this is a *complete handbook* on this whole business of writing and selling greeting cards. It contains everything you need to know to get started now in this business. All *you* need to use this information and become a selling professional greeting card writer is determination, discipline, guts, and a bit of talent.

HJC

Acknowledgments

My thanks are gratefully given to the following greeting card companies for the use of many of their best-selling verses and gags. Without their courteous and generous permission and help, a book of this nature would never have been possible.

Barker Greeting Card Company
Cincinnati, Ohio

Buzza-Cardozo
Anaheim, California

Gibson Greeting Cards, Inc.
Cincinnati, Ohio

Hallmark Cards, Inc.
Kansas City, Missouri

Charm Craft Publishing Co.
Brooklyn, New York

Keep 'N Touch
Greeting Cards, Inc.
Framingham, Massachusetts

Rust Craft Greeting Cards, Inc.
Dedham, Massachusetts

The House of Oz, Inc.
Clifton, New Jersey

The Paramount Line, Inc.
Pawtucket, Rhode Island

Vagabond Creations
West Carrollton, Ohio

My thanks also to the Barker Greeting Card Company for three years of invaluable experience; to Harry Onufrock, President of Barker, for his guidance and counsel; to Ken Berry, Creative Director of Barker, for his patience and generous sharing of his creative experience; to Moe Becker, Sandy Brewer, Howard Garrison, Morris Gordon, Joe Harris, Bob Levine, Bob Lloyd, and Ted Touster for their unfailing help; and to Jean Scholten who started me, Becky Saylor who was in the middle, and Nancy Suprenant who finished me.

Thanks also to Hal Chadwick, Margaret Gould, Lee Greenwell, and George Wilson for suggestions and help on portions of this book.

HJC

Contents

magazine. Writing conventional verse in an unconventional way. Examples, examples, examples. Verses without feeling. Sub-titles. Some personal thoughts.

Something inspired. Old proverbs and familiar writings. Examples, examples, examples. The first inspirational verse I ever wrote. The Magic of Prayer, a powerful verse. The magic. More examples. Inspirational verses are from the heart.

Neither fish nor fowl. Writing techniques. Text and illustration. Think visually. What's in a name. Examples, examples, examples.

The pay is good. It's fun. Verse cards vs. activity cards. The age series. Several kinds of activity cards. Where do ideas come from? Ideas from your children. Children's games and books. Illustrating your ideas. The age groups. A special way of getting ideas. Giving instructions on your cards. Some personal philosophy. Branching out to other fields.

The hard work of being funny. What is a humorous card? Something for your readers to identify with. Help for you. Humor formulas. Verse in humorous cards. Some final thoughts.

find switchable material. Humor formulas: Exaggeration, Insult, Reverse, Combinations, Definitions, Misunderstanding, Literal, Play-on-words, Repetition, Whimsy, Topical, Zany. A personal formula.

Don't just send it off. Is your idea ready for market? A check list for your ideas. Some forms to submit ideas on. To illustrate or not to illustrate? A simple way to learn to illustrate your ideas. Stamps, envelopes, and other things. "Dear Editor:" Rights and wrongs. How many ideas should I keep in the mail? What if the editor says to me . . .? How long to submit an idea before giving up on it. Editors and you.

As important as writing the card. Some quick and simple methods. Coding your ideas. Keeping track of where your ideas have been. Keeping track of ideas you are submitting. Sending queries about ideas out too long. What to do about batches that come back with ideas missing. If you've run out of companies and your idea hasn't sold. Filing seasonal ideas and ideas that haven't sold. What to do if you find a published card identical with one you've just sold. Releases, expenses, and taxes.

Chapter I

Greeting Cards...What Are They?

by H. Joseph Chadwick

The dictionary on my desk defines a greeting as an "Expression of kindness or joy; salutation at meeting; a compliment from one absent." But to greeting card companies, a greeting is plainly and simply a "me-to-you-message."

Remember those four words: ME-TO-YOU-MESSAGE! They are the four most important words you'll ever see or hear in your greeting card writing career. Remember them and use them in every greeting card you write, and all your troubles will be checks. Forget them, and you'll be able to paper your house with rejection slips. Now let's take a look at the different types of greeting cards that you'll be meeting, both in this book and in your writing. Then after we've done that, we'll take a look at what happens to an idea you've just sold.

Greeting cards can be broken down into six basic types: *conventional, inspirational, informal, juvenile, humorous,* and *studio. Conventional* cards are also known as *general* cards, just as *informals* are sometimes called *cutes* and *studio* cards are often referred to as *contemporary* cards. But don't let the basic names confuse you, you'll soon learn to recognize the six basic types regardless of what they're called. Let's consider each type separately.

Conventional cards are the backbone of the greeting card industry. They put the meat and potatoes on the table. Recent figures indicate that over 10,000,000 conventional greeting cards are sold every day of the year. To satisfy this insatiable appetite, practically all greeting card companies that publish conventional cards are constantly in the market for good verses. For these, they pay anywhere from 50¢ to $3.00 a line, depending on the size of the company and the quality of the verse.

The types of verses used in conventional cards range from those on the highly formal cards that might say nothing more than *Happy Birthday and best wishes for the coming year,* to the extremely sentimental verse that might say:

TO MY WIFE
I love sharing Christmas
The way we do, Dear,
I love being with you
To start the New Year,
I love you for doing
The sweet things you do
That make me so thankful
I share life with YOU!

Inspirational cards were at one time simply slightly more poetic and religious sounding cards *within* the conventional card line. But in recent years, because of the great success of inspirational cards written by Helen Farries at Buzza-Cardozo, Helen Steiner Rice at Gibson, and inspirational promotions brought out by most of the major companies, the inspirational card has become a power unto itself, and is becoming more and more separated from the regular conventional line.

On the average, inspirational verse will bring the writer more money per line than regular conventional verse. This is because good inspirational verse is harder to write. Since the purpose of inspirational verse is to inspire, it is usually highly poetical and almost Biblical in nature. For this reason, there is a fine line between *good* inspirational verse that can send a thrill through you, and bad inspirational verse that is over-dramatic and corny. It takes an excellent writer to jump the line into truly inspirational verse. Here is an example of some by Helen Farries:

I THOUGHT OF YOU AND SAID A LITTLE PRAYER

This morning when I wakened
And saw the sun above,
I softly said, "Good Morning, Lord,
Bless everyone I love!"

Right away I thought of you
And said a little prayer
That he would bless you specially
And keep you free from care . . .

I thought of all the happiness
A day could hold in store,
And wished it all for you because
No one deserves it more!

I felt so warm and good inside,
My heart was all aglow . . .
I know God heard my prayer for you,
He hears them all you know!

Informal cards, often called *cutes,* appear to be offshoots of studio cards. They are softer in humor and more sentimental than studios, but they are in general written in prose and follow basically the same humor formulas that studios do. Since in the beginning of their development, studio cards appealed mainly to men, it would appear that informal cards were originally women's answer to studio cards. However, now that studio humor is becoming softer and less slammy and risque, the line between informal cards and studio cards is getting thinner and thinner. And you will often find a studio card with a gag that by all rights and formulas should be classified as an informal.

In most cases, the rate of payment for informal ideas is about the same as for studio ideas, although it might be less in some instances, if the informal idea is going to be used on a lower price card. When reading informal cards, look for the often used play-on-words, the tie-in with the illustration, and the soft humor. For example:

> (Cute toy horse on cover)
> Forget your birthday? . . .
> . . . NEIGH! Have a happy!

Juvenile cards are written to be sent *to children,* usually *by adults.* Some juveniles are nothing but a design and verse, while others are elaborate games and mechanical toys, and some are even complete story books. Although at one time most card companies put out some juvenile cards, they are fast becoming the exclusive property of the major companies. The cost of producing juvenile greeting cards is high, because they must be elaborate to compete with all the juvenile toys, games, and books on the market.

The pay for juvenile card ideas is as high as it is for studio ideas, and is sometimes higher. Juvenile story books may earn the writer $100 or more a book. In general, however, the pay for juvenile ideas will run from about $20 to $50, especially for the activity ideas, like this one:

> HI THERE! MERRY CHRISTMAS!
>
> No need to wait till Christmas,
> Start having fun right now.
> Play Santa's brand-new *bingo* game,
> Inside tells you how . . .
> (Inside the card is a spinner and
> a bingo game that uses toys instead
> of numbers.)

Humorous cards, like juveniles, range from simply design and verse to elaborate mechanicals. In general, the verse is tied tightly to the illustration, and the card gains its humor both from the verse and from the humorous illustration. Often, illustrations of animals are used to represent humans, just as is frequently done on juvenile cards. The pay for humorous cards is about the same as for juveniles and studio cards, depending, of course, on how elaborate the humorous card is.

The humor used in humorous cards is seldom contemporary, although it may be based upon topical subjects. Usually, the humor is more amusing than hilarious, more cute than contemporary. For example:

> I hope your day is happy,
> I hope your day is pleasant.
> And what is more, I also hope . . .
> . . . You didn't expect a present!

Studio cards are the thigh-slappers of the greeting card industry, the black sheep of the family, the young upstarts that dared to grow up, the cards that were not spoken of in the same breath as regular cards. Studio card designers and writers were considered to be somewhat strange and queer acting and not to be associated with by regular greeting card folks. No one ever thought that the small, make-shift departments, usually hidden behind the elevator shaft, would ever have the effrontery to make money for the companies. But they did, even though the companies hated to admit they even made those *studio* things.

This was, as the Bible says, *in the beginning,* of course. Nowadays, each is proud and happy to admit that it was *he* who originated studio cards.

What was the first studio card? The closest rumor seems to be that it was a card that showed a little old man sitting inside a wooden box that was turned up on its end . . . the man was huddled up and staring out at the reader . . . there were no words on the cover, only the design. Inside, the card said: *People are no damn good!*

Another interesting rumor is how studio cards got the long, modern, rectangular shape they have. It seems, rumor says, that the originator of studio cards was strapped for money, and he or she or it found that the cheapest envelopes available at the time were the long business-size envelopes. So cards were made to fit the envelopes. Thus, the modern rectangular shape of studio cards resulted from nothing more than economy . . . rumor says.

But one thing that *is* modern about studio cards is its humor. If you were looking for a handle for the type of humor in studio cards, it would have to be contemporary humor, the *now* humor, humor that is happening, that is living and breathing every day. Studio card humor is probably more representative of the *people's* humor than all the comedians, joke books, movies, and whathaveyou's put together, because all the other types of humor are fed to people. Such humor is what somebody, somewhere decided to give us. But with studio cards we can pick and choose and buy only the humor we like! So studio cards are a direct reflection of what you and I are laughing at today.

> COVER: You're like a vintage wine,
> you get nicer with age . . .
> INSIDE: . . . but your keg is starting
> to swell . . .
> HAPPY BIRTHDAY

Now that you know the kind of cards you'll be writing ideas for, let's follow an idea from your house to the greeting card store. Just for the sake of assuming, let's assume that you write studio card ideas. (We're ignoring staff writers, by the way, because we all know they're there and that free-lance writers have to suffer them and compete with them . . . and that's a fact of life.)

You start with a blank piece of paper on your desk or kitchen table. Now there is nothing more awesome, more fearful, more dreaded by any writer than a blank piece of paper. It conjures, teases, demands, taunts . . . and more often than we like to think about, it just sits there and defies us. Yet, each and every time, we have to start with a blank piece of paper. (A favorite retort for know-nothing critics of something you've written is, "Where were you when there was nothing on that piece of paper?!?")

Finally, after going through all the techniques and methods and doing all the things that get you started, an idea begins to take shape somewhere in a dim, seldom used braincell that has been storing up bits of information waiting for just this moment to release them. You pull, you pray, you tease the words out one at a time, and timorously put them down on that screaming blank piece of paper in front of you. This time, the words come out good. So you revise them, type them, make a copy for your file, and then, along with several others that you have prayed into existence, you send the idea off to an editor who sits somewhere in Cardland playing god with your brainchildren, deciding coldly which of them he will reject — and you with them — and which he will give life to.

You wait and try not to think about how many days and hours and minutes it's been since you mailed your ideas to him. Then one day your return envelope comes back — the return envelope that all editors insist you send along with your submissions, and which always gives you the feeling of carrying the rope to your own hanging — and in the envelope, hidden among rejected ideas, is a short, terse note saying: *I am buying your idea B-RTY for $35. Our check will be along in about a week.*

You rejoice! All is right with your world! You love the editor and the mailman! Tomorrow you may hate them both and curse them into Hades, but today you love them, and you face the new blank piece of paper with renewed vigor and confidence — at least for the first ten minutes. And maybe during one of those long pauses, when nothing seems to be coming, when you *just know* you've written everything there is to be written, maybe you stop for a moment and wonder why the editor bought your last idea, and *what* he did with it.

When the editor got your envelope full of ideas, it was just one envelope out of the hundred or more he gets each week, and your idea was just one of the more than 1,000 ideas he reads each week. But though he read through your ideas in a hurry (he has to just to keep up with the mail!), his experienced eye told him that one of your ideas had a certain originality and appeal to it, and so he marked the idea and put your envelope into a special *hold* file. By the end of the week, he had accumulated a considerable number of *holds,* and so he set up a *product* (or *line planning*) *meeting* for that coming Monday.

At the meeting were several staff members: the Art Director was there, as he always is; the Sales Manager and his new assistant; the Creative Director, who was recently made Vice President; the Company Manager; two of the squinty-eyed people from Line Planning; a couple of twitching pencils from Merchandising; and even the President decided to attend this meeting, which sort of made the editor's day.

He laid out on the conference table all the ideas he had been holding, along with voting sheets for everyone to use, and then sat back on the edge of his nerves while they all looked and snorted and twitched the corners of their mouths at each of the ideas he had hopefully held from the thousands his burning, sandpaper-filled eyes had read. Then they discussed the ideas, told him why his judgment was poor, hinted that maybe it was even lousy, admitted that he had accidentally held a few good ones, and agreed as to how it would probably be all right . . . since he couldn't seem to do any better . . . if he bought these few ideas out of the hundreds he held . . . and could he get them at half price? Or, at least, it *seemed* as though that was what they were saying. But editors get quickly cynical and seldom hear or see things rationally.

So now the meeting was over, and on his desk were the ideas he was buying, your idea among them. When he got to your idea, he decided on how much it was worth (you got more because of that attachment you put on it . . . remember?!). Then he typed out the short, terse note that put some well-deserved money into your pocketbook and made you kiss the mailman (or at least shake his hand). The other ideas, the ones his committee turned down, had to be returned to the writers, and because he had held the ideas, he felt he owed at least a personal note to them rather than just a printed rejection slip. So he wrote a note to each writer, telling them their idea had at least got to the meeting. He was hoping this would take some of the sting off the rejection and so keep them submitting ideas to him.

After he sent out all the notes, and did all the things that would ultimately result in your getting the actual check, he went over the accepted ideas one at a time, working them into their final form. When he got to your idea, he rewrote it slightly, put a *Happy Birthday* on the outside where you had forgot it, corrected a misspelled word (that one you always have trouble with!), did a few other things to it to get the text in just the right form, and then since he had an immediate requirement for the idea, he sent it on to the Art Director, along with several other ideas that completed his requirements for that week (Thank God!).

The Art Director then called in a staff artist and assigned your idea to him. Together they discussed several possible designs and colors, and then the artist went off to his spot in the wall to do those mysterious things greeting card artists do. After a few hours, maybe even a day, the artist came back to the Director with several rough designs. The director liked one of the roughs that showed a cute little character in a blue hat and pants and red shirt and shoes. So the artist went back to his drawing board to draw up the finished art work.

First he made a complete black and white drawing (such as in cartoons) of the design, and then he made an acetate (clear plastic sheet) layover for each of the colors in the design. To make the layovers, the artist taped a clear piece of acetate the size of the card over the black and white drawing. Then he used an opaque material to carefully and exactly fill in the areas of the acetate that covered the character's hat and pants, which were to be printed the same color. After that, he laid another piece of acetate exactly over the first one, and filled in with the opaque material the area on the acetate that covered the shirt and shoes, which were to be printed a different color from the hat and pants. Had there been a third color, he would have laid another sheet of clear acetate over the first two and opaqued-in the area of the third color.

Now that he had finished the art work, the artist gave the design to a letterer who then hand-lettered all of the text. After this was done, all of the design work went back to the art director and the editor for a final check of the design and text. Since both were okay, the design was then sent to the engraver, who made plates for the black and white design, each of the colors, and the lettering. The plates were then sent to the Printing Department where they were set up on a printing press.

Twenty-thousand cards were printed of your idea, and then they were all folded in a strange looking machine and sent up to the Finishing Department. There, highly skilled women glued the attachment on each card. If the card had been a mechanical, it would have been die-cut after printing, and then all the various parts would have been sent to Finishing where the women would have glued them all together into a working mechanical card. Now the card was packed into boxes of twelve and stored, there to await shipment to hundreds of stores throughout the country.

But before a card can be shipped, it has to be sold. So at some stage, a number of cards were sent to what we will call the Sampling Department. There, your card and several dozen others were packed into boxes and sent to the company salesmen. When the salesmen received their *samples,* they put them into their sample cases and immediately started showing them to their customers: the store owners and buyers. The customers ordered the number of boxes they wanted of each card, and every evening the salesmen sent their orders in to the Sales Department at the home office. In a very short time, the first orders were on their way to the customers, your card among them.

When the first store owner received his order, he unpacked the cards and put them in the card racks for his customers. Just a few hours after he put the cards up, a beautiful lady walked in, picked up one of your cards, laughed, and said "This would be just *perfect* for Harriet . . . it's *her* all over!" She rushed to the counter, paid for your card, and hurried out the door to send it to Harriet who lived in California and would be 29 (she says) on Saturday.

So the blank piece of paper you started with, the paper you put words, humor, and sentiment upon, those little bits and pieces of yourself, has reached its ultimate goal, bringing happiness, gladness, maybe a tear or a laugh to not only one, but thousands of people all over the world.

Through the medium of greeting cards, you, the writer, have reached out from your desk or kitchen table, and touched the heart, mind, and soul of another human being.

In so doing, you have enriched his life, and yours.

Think about it.

It's kind of a nice talent to have.

Chapter II

Conventional Verse: The Sentimental Favorite

by Chris FitzGerald

After writing in the greeting card field for over eight years, I'm apt to forget a few things. I'm very willing to forget, for instance, how far off base I was the first time I sat down to write a greeting card verse.

I put a lot of effort into that first little work of art — a sweetheart birthday verse, if I remember correctly. It had continuity, a certain music, imagery, subtlety of thought — and it was awful! It was half verse and half poetry, one fourth commercial and three fourths personal, and 100 percent useless.

I made the mistake many beginners make. I had read the ordinary, trite verses that had been published, and I thought to myself, "Let's give those tired editors something with a little quality and watch them light up." Well, they didn't light up, and I had an advantage over most of you: I could see the extent to which they did not light up. As a management trainee in the editorial department of American Greetings Corporation, I was expected to learn to write verse so that I could one day manage writers more effectively. I had a couple of very good teachers; and, in fact, they did their job so well that I became more interested in writing than in managing (although it took me seven years of combined writing and administrative work at American and Gibson Greeting Cards before I became a full-fledged freelance writer).

With the advantage of day-to-day tutorship of experienced writers and editors, I could write garbage and be told so immediately with varying degrees of tact or candor.

You can go on writing garbage forever and possibly never be told — except, of course, by the absence of sales.

I was in daily contact with my sometimes despairing teachers. They could afford to teach me gradually, be patient with me, lead me kindly.

We — you and I, in the context of this chapter — don't have the time for such amenities. I shall therefore take a chance with you and — hoping that you have some spunk, a sense of detachment, and a sense of humor — tell you that your verse (greeting card verse, that is) probably stinks.

I really would rather have the time with you to be as gentle as my mentors were with me, but we haven't got time. In all probability, your stuff is as bad as mine was when I started. But that's no reason for discouragement. I learned, and you can learn.

You can learn, first, to gain a respect for greeting card verse as it is. You can make improvements, yes, but only from the inside out. You have to learn to write trite verse before you can write quality verse. That statement might not sit well with your sensibilities, but that's telling it like it is, believe me.

First off, every neophyte must rid himself of the notion that greeting card verse is poetry. It is not poetry. It is ordinary speech expressed in the framework of meter and rhyme. The thing to remember is that it is, first and foremost, ordinary speech, and only secondarily, versified speech.

> Hope you're feeling better
> And it won't be very long
> Before you're on your feet again,
> Completely well and strong.

Trite? Hackneyed? Maybe so. But it gets across a very basic message, and I would guess that every company has this verse practically verbatim in its Illness line. Match up that verse (you'll agree it isn't poetry) with an attractive design, and it will sell to thousands of people who want to say just that and no more to someone on the sick list.

You wouldn't be able to sell that verse to an editor, however, because he (or, probably, she) would figure it was just *too* ordinary to be purchased from a free-lance writer. He might accept it from a staff trainee and say that it shows good basic thinking. Before long, however, he would expect a little more imagination from his budding artist. Maybe something like this:

> Hope you're feeling better
> And before much time goes by
> Your friends are once more favored
> By the twinkle in your eye.

This verse is somewhat more limited than the previous one, in that it contains not only a wish, but also an implied compliment (the likeability of the receiver) and a word ("favored") which is not universally used in everyday speech. But it's a little different from the run of the mill and, therefore, would stand a good chance of catching the tired eye of an editor.

To get back to the point, however, it is important to express yourself in the down-to-earth, everyday language of the people, because that is the language the people prefer in their greeting cards.

This brings up an important point. You must always remember that you are writing for someone else. When a little lady in Rolla, Missouri, buys a birthday card for her sister in Oklahoma City, she considers the message *hers*. From the publisher's viewpoint, a card is successful if enough people can identify so completely with what it says and how it says it that they consider it *their own expression*.

There are no by-lines on greeting cards (with the exception of some inspirational or special numbers). If the hand of the writer is too evident in his work, it will stand in the way of the person-to-person communication that people look for in a greeting card.

This does not mean that a writer can't have style. It only means that his style must not get in the way of personal communication. If his style, on the other hand, helps communication, then it serves a real purpose.

The best place to observe greeting card writing is, of course, in greeting cards. This seems so obvious that it's hardly worth men-tioning, but I have observed that many aspiring card writers have little patience when it comes to studying published cards. They look at a few — and these only superficially — and can hardly wait to write *much better verses of their own*. This is only natural, but if you really want to learn this business you have to read, read, and read greeting cards. It helps to be on friendly terms with the folks who run your local card shop. (Buy a few cards once in a while, and hopefully they won't mind your doing research.)

It might be well at this point to make it clear that I am not suggesting that you plagiarize existing cards. Imitation may be the sincerest form of flattery, but that kind of flattery will get you nowhere. Read cards to observe idea content, verse pattern, writing style, rhyme schemes and the like; but when you sit down to write, come up with your own verse. This doesn't mean that you can't paraphrase an existing verse. Paraphrasing — saying the same thing in different words — is actually a good way for a beginner to go about learning technique. Eventually, you will come up with ideas that you yourself would like to say in a card, and the verses created in this way will most likely be your best.

To show you how paraphrasing works, let's imagine that you begin with a published verse that goes like this:

> Just a little passing thought
> To give your heart a lift:

> The joy of having friends like you
> Is life's most precious gift.

No great model to paraphrase, but it does contain a good basic idea: the gift of friendship. It also suggests that the receiver is in need of being cheered up, but we'll pass over that idea in the rewrite. You will note that in this verse there is no use of the first person (no "I"). This is more often the case than not in greeting cards — so that a given card may be sent by one *or more* persons. However, in your paraphrase let's say that you make it an "I" verse, especially since this *is* a friendship card, and a good proportion of such cards use the first person singular.

Anyway, after some head-scratching and paper-scratching you come up with this spin-off version:

> Among the finest gifts of life
> Is friendship, good and true —
> The kind of friendship I have found
> So nicely in you.

Pretty good for a new writer, but it does have its faults. For one thing, the last line is rather short — in fact, it's missing a whole beat, or foot, in the meter. It also contains a pet peeve of many editors in its use of inverted word order in the second line, where the adjectives ("good and true") are placed behind the word they modify ("friendship"). Back to the writing board.

After a few whacks at it, you take care of the first objection by changing the last two lines to read:

> The special kind of friendship
> That I value so in you.

The inversion is not objectionable in this case, so you could consider the verse finished, and you might even be able to sell it. Maybe.

Then again you might try a different tack and rewrite your lines something like these:

> Friendship is life's finest gift,
> And from my point of view
> No friendship could be nicer
> Than the one I share with you.

Now you're getting somewhere. As you can readily see, one idea leads to another. You start by paraphrasing, you sample ideas, accepting and rejecting words and phrases on the basis of whether they fit or not.

Finding ideas and words that fit is where craftsmanship comes in. Once you determine what you want to say — and in this regard, it is best to stick to one basic idea — you must choose your words to do several things at the same time:

(1) Your idea must be expressed as a complete idea; it must have a beginning, a middle, and an end.

(2) There must be coherence in your verse. Every line must be linked logically and smoothly with its neighbors.

(3) Your expressions, as stressed before, must be conversational. High-flown language rarely comes off successfully in greeting card writing.

(4) You must write with emphasis — and something else: enthusiasm. It's necessary to create interest in that all-important first line. From that point on, writing your verse is a matter of developing your idea and bringing it to a peak of emphasis in the last line. Occasionally you will find that you have shot your wad too early in the verse, and whatever you say after that point sounds like an after-thought.

(5) You must do all of the above and at the same time make everything come out right in the meter-and-rhyme department. The ability to versify comes naturally to a few; for most of us, it is an acquired skill, and the only way to develop it is to keep working at it until you find yourself thinking in meter and anticipating rhymes.

With regard to rhymes, it is important to stress that your rhyming words must fit the sense of what you want to say. It should not appear that you are saying things just to make rhymes. Rhyming, after all, is an adornment of language; but language, first and foremost, must communicate. Adornment, in other words, is secondary to meaning.

You will find in your study of existing cards that relatively few rhyme sounds are actually used. Here is a listing of the more frequently used rhyming words:

SOUNDS	KEY WORDS
ad	add, bad, Dad, glad, had, sad, mad, lad (rare)
after	after, laughter
air	care, compare, pair, prayer, where, everywhere, there, anywhere
ake	make, take, cake, mistake, break, sake
ame	same, blame, name, aim, claim, came
and	hand, understand, planned, stand
ar	are, far, star
art	heart, start, part, impart (sometimes acceptable)
ast	last, past, passed, fast
ate	great, date, late, state, wait, congratulate, create, hesitate, anticipate, celebrate
ay	day, way, stay, say, convey, may
aze	days, ways, praise
ear	dear, clear, hear, here, near, sincere, year, cheer
earn	earn, concern, return, learn, turn, yearn
ee	be, me, see
eel	feel, real, conceal, reveal
eem	dream, seem
eet	sweet, complete, beat, meet, repeat, greet
el	tell, swell, well, excel, bell
end	send, friend, end, mend (accident), spend, depend, extend, blend

SOUNDS	KEY WORDS
ent	sent, went, content, meant, extent
est	best, expressed, blessed, guessed, rest, happiest
et	yet, get, forget, met, regret, bet
eze	these, please, ease
I	high, by, buy, sigh, eye, why, fly, guy, I, sky, deny, reply, try
ice	nice, twice, suffice, advice
ick	sick, quick, trick, stick
ide	pride, confide, denied, side, abide, hide, guide, tried, bride, stride, tied, wide, decide, supplied
ife	life, wife
ile	smile, while, aisle, style
ime	time, rhyme, sublime
in	been, in, spin, begin
ind	find, mind, kind, signed
ine	fine, sign, line, mine
ing	bring, thing, spring (Easter)
irl	girl, whirl, curl
iss	this, kiss, bliss, miss, Sis
ite	night, sight, might, delight, light, right
iv	live, give, forgive
ize	surprise, eyes, rise, guys, wise, qualifies
o	go, grow, know, so, show
old	old, told, bold
oo	you, too, to, two, view, new, knew, do, true, who, through
or	more, before, for, store, door
own	own, shown, alone
ow	now, somehow, how, bow
other	other, mother, another, brother
oy	boy, joy, enjoy, toy

SOUNDS	KEY WORDS
un	done, son, sun, one, someone, anyone, everyone, fun, begun, run
um	come, some, from
uv	love, of, above

This is just a partial list, of course, but I would venture to say that at least 85 percent of all greeting card verses make use of the above rhyming words. Furthermore, there is a preponderance of *oo, ay,* and *ear* rhymes because of the heavy usage of such words as *day, way, say, you, do, too, dear, year,* and *sincere* in greeting situations. Editors get a little tired of encountering the same rhyming words all the time, and yet they accept them as naturals in the language of greetings.

Fresh rhyme schemes are welcomed, of course, as long as the resulting expression is natural and unforced. This brings to mind the studio card in the Gibson line that goes something like this: (front) *"I'm writing you a poem for your birthday . . ."* (inside) *"What rhymes with BLOCKHEAD?"* The point is, don't force yourself into impossible situations by using hard-to-rhyme words in the rhyming positions.

Be sure you have a true rhyme, too. Assonance (roughly approximate sounds) may be acceptable in poetry, but a greeting card verse demands close rhyming. You can get away with a *you-new* scheme, even though a purist might contest it, but you can't make *wind* and *find* and *line* rhyme under any circumstances.

Remember, too, that rhymes occur between stressed syllables (and in so-called feminine rhymes between sets of stressed and unstressed syllables — e.g., *light-hearted* and *started*). The words *wish* and *stylish* don't rhyme because the "ish" sound in the one case is stressed, and in the other, unstressed.

You have to make allowances, too, for regional differences in pronunciation. If you were a native Bostonian, for example, you might be inclined to rhyme *year* and *idea,* but even the folks at Rust Craft (Dedham, Mass.) wouldn't let you get away with it. On the other hand, even though you'd be correct in rhyming *yours* and *endures,* many editors would shy away from this usage because of the inclination of Midwesterners and others to make *yours* rhyme with *stores.*

I once rhymed *Mom* and *calm* in a verse and was surprised when at length the verse was purchased. The words do rhyme — in the dictionary at least — but the editor has to decide if the rhyme also exists in the consumer's use of the language.

Most greeting card verses follow this rhyme pattern for four lines: *x a x a* (that is, second and fourth lines rhyming; first and third lines not rhyming). The typical eight-line verse follows this pattern: *x a x a x b x b* (odd-numbered lines not rhyming; second and fourth lines making one rhyme; sixth and eighth another rhyme).

Less frequently, you find verses based on an *a a b b* and *a a b b c c d d* format; editors refer to this as "couplet style."

The most frequently used meter in greeting card verse is a rather sing-songy iambic form that alternates from four feet (that's metric feet) in the odd-numbered lines to three feet in the even-numbered lines. If you remember your lessons in scanning poetry, you know that a foot contains one strong beat, or stressed syllable, and one or more light beats or unstressed syllables (with the exception of the spondee meter, in which theoretically there are no unstressed syllables). Reducing it to something like Morse code, the basic iambic 4/3/4/3 verse form goes like this: In our Morse code, a stressed syllable is —, and an unstressed syllable is u.)

$$u - / u - / u - / u -$$
$$u - / u - / u -$$
$$u - / u - / u - / u -$$
$$u - / u - / u -$$

Here is a sympathy verse ("From Both of Us" category) that I sold to Hallmark; in it you will find the above pattern followed exactly in the first lines and approximately in the last four lines:

> We want to send our sympathy
> But find it hard to say
> The kind of thing that possibly
> Might comfort you today,
> And yet perhaps just knowing
> That our thoughts are with you now
> Will bring you consolation
> And will lift your heart somehow.

The variation in the last four lines consists of carrying over the stressed syllable that belongs at the end of the fifth and seventh lines and placing it at the beginning of the sixth and eighth lines. Like so:

$$u — / u — / u — / u$$
$$— / u — / u — / u —$$
$$u — / u — / u — / u$$
$$— / u — / u — / u —$$

This variation is perfectly acceptable, and it may occur once, twice, or as many times as you want it to in a verse. Just remember, you're borrowing a stressed syllable from the odd-numbered line and giving it to the even-numbered line. It doesn't work too well the other way; that is, you can't usually take the initial unstressed syllable that belongs to the even-numbered line and carry it back to the end of the preceding line. If you did, you'd end up with something like this:

> I'm wishing you a happy birthday
> Filled with everything
> That you in your own fondest wishes
> Hope the day will bring.

It's passable, maybe, but a little awkward in that the odd-numbered lines are so long in comparison with the even-numbered lines.

Another common variation is the omission of the initial un-stressed syllable in a line. Instead of saying "I'm wishing you a happy day," you may start with a stressed syllable and say, "Wish-ing you a happy day." It's still a four-foot iambic line, but you've omitted the unstressed half of the initial foot.

In like manner, you may drop the final stress on the odd-numbered lines if you wish. For example:

> Here's wishing you a birthday
> That's happy through and through
> For you're so nice, that's just the kind
> That you're entitled to!

The rest of the verse is standard, but the first line is lacking a final stress, and this is permissible. Some editors feel that once you deviate from pattern you must stick to the deviation all the way through, but I can't agree with that position. On the con-trary, I feel that variations should be used to break up an other-wise too rigid pattern. It takes skill, of course, to know *where* to vary the meter by adding an extra unstressed syllable or by leaving out a beat. You have to learn the standard pattern first, and then your ear will tell you where you may and where you may not alter the pattern.

The iambic meter is adaptable to many moods. It can be formal or informal, serious or light-hearted, masculine or feminine in appeal. The same meter, for example, that was followed in the sympathy verse above was used in this get-well verse, also pub-lished by Hallmark:

> Please concentrate on happy things
> To keep your spirits high . . .
> Think of things like tulips
> Throwing kisses to the sky . . .

Think of cuddly kittens . . .
Children dancing in the hills . . .
Butterflies a-flutter
Over waking daffodils . . .
Curly headed schoolboys
Singing slightly out of tune . . .
But most of all, please concentrate
On feeling better soon!

This verse, by the way, illustrates that you can get a little poetic once in a while in greeting cards. You'll note, however, that the imagery has a practical purpose ("to keep your spirits high") and that in the final lines of the verse the purpose for sending the card is plainly stated. The "poetry" is there only insofar as it supports this fundamental message.

Another effective, if less versatile, meter for greeting cards is the dactyl, whose basic foot consists of a stressed syllable followed by two unstressed syllables (— u u). Related to this is the anapest meter which is just the reverse (u u —). Either may be used to good effect where a light, tripping cadence is desired. Note the lilting effect of the meter in this Christmas verse:

Everything Christmasy,
Everything bright,
Everything merry
From morning till night —
That's what you're wished
At this time of good cheer,
Along with life's best
Through a wonderful year!

— u u / — u u
— u u / —
— u u / — u
u / — u u / —

— u u / —
u u / — u u / —
u — / u u —
u u — / u u —

As you can see, there is some mixing of dactyl and anapest in this verse; the first six lines are dactyl, and the last two are anapest. In the first foot of line seven one of the light stresses is missing. This is not uncommon. In the dactyl section you see that the last foot of the even-numbered lines consist of the one stressed syllable only. This is quite normal; in fact, since rhymes usually fall on final stressed syllables, this is the standard pattern. You could, however, have a feminine rhyme, and in this case the last foot would be like so: — u (minute, in it), or even — u u (scenery, greenery).

I don't want to get too hung up on this subject of meter, because it can *sound* very confusing, when really all you need is to read a lot of verses and have a fairly good sense of rhythm, and you'll get it. Some understanding of basic principles, though, is helpful.

Economy of speech is an important ingredient of greeting cards. A four-line verse usually consists of about 22 words; an eight-line verse, believe it or not, is double that number. In the space of these few words, then, you must choose your words carefully. Any wasted word slows down the movement of the verse and causes a loss of emphasis. Any word that doesn't ring true will create a reaction against the whole verse in the mind of the ultimate buyer (and in the mind of the editor, too).

In most verses an informal pattern of speech should be maintained; therefore, you should use contractions where these are normally used in ordinary speech. ("I'm thinking of you, Honey, and I don't mind saying so" instead of "I am thinking of you, Honey, and I do not mind saying so.") Sometimes, for the sake of meter you will *want* to sacrifice natural speech for speech that fits, but you'll be making a mistake. Keep working at it until it really "fits" — in the sense of a total "fit" of meaning, naturalness, and meter.

Writing verse is an art for perfectionists. A verse that has one weak line, or one weak expression, is an "unfinished" verse; it's a verse that a writer struggled with and gave up on. You will find yourself confronted with verses that you can't finish to your satisfaction, and when this happens, it's better to set the verse aside for a while. Later inspection will often reveal the answer to the problem you couldn't cope with earlier. Or you'll see that the problem is as knotty as ever and toss the verse in the waste basket as "one that got away." It pays to be tough on yourself. After all, your work is your representative in the offices of the editors, and you deserve to be well-represented.

On the other hand, there's a limit to which perfectionism should be carried (and that is far short of perfect). You should rely on your own taste, but also recognize that you are not the only judge of your work. Something you don't like might very well appeal to other people — including, hopefully, at least one editor on your routing list. Remember, too, that what one editor finds unacceptable, another may find quite acceptable. Don't give up easily in your bid for acceptance.

Don't expect your work to be grabbed up immediately, by the way. Editors are human — contrary to belief in some quarters — and they like to feel confidence in you as a contributor before committing themselves to any large-scale purchases of your work. They want to see that you are going to be a steady contributor operating as a true professional. Some editors will buy very little of your work until a year or two have gone by. It's like any other business: regardless of the quality of your work, people — in this case, editors — want to do business with a winner. And it takes time for anyone to establish himself as a true professional.

Chapter III

Conventional Verse: Getting Specific

by Chris FitzGerald

Writing greeting card verse is a two-level proposition. On one level, you must learn the writing style of greeting cards; on another level, you must learn the do's and don't's in the various categories of cards that are published. It is these do's and don't's that we are concerned with in this chapter.

Greeting cards fall into two major categories: Everyday and Seasonal. In the listings that follow, the comments given in the everyday category usually apply to the corresponding captions in the Seasonal category. The same is true for the *special captions.* These are non-relative captions such as: From Both, Sweetheart, and Honey.

Here is the listing of Everyday and Seasonal captions. It is not a complete list, but it will give you a good idea of the large number of captions published, and give you guidelines.

Everyday Captions

Birthday

General: A wide range of ideas, moods and styles are found in this caption. Almost anything goes: formal, noncommittal, semi-sentimental, sentimental. Ideas include: wish, compliment, thinking of you, affection, comments on youthfulness. No restrictions on meter. Length: mostly 4 and 8 lines, but longer lengths (12, 16, 20 and up) are occasionally used. Moods range from light to serious, straightforward to whimsical. Write for all ages and types of people. Most buyers are women, but publishers include in their lines cards that represent varying degrees of feminity and masculinity. There are cards that women send to men or women, cards that women send to women, that women send to men, that men send to men or women, etc. These cards are not labeled as such, but editors attempt to keep a balance along these lines.

Birthday—Special Captions

Sweetheart: Cards for unmarried or married couples, young or old, together or apart. Degree of sentiment ranges from semi-sentimental to very sentimental. Ideas: love, affection, memories, wishes, sharing, dreams, compliments, thinking of you. Light or serious approach. No restrictions on "I" verses. Mostly 8-line verses, some 4's, a few "specials" at 12, 16, or more lines. All meters. Avoid references to specific features (blue eyes, lovely face, etc.), but feel free to refer to general features (your face, your eyes, your smile). The word *Sweetheart* is ideal for versification: it is a good rhyming word (start, apart, part, impart, smart), and it's one of those rare words that permits the accent to fall on either the first or second syllable, depending on its position in a line or verse ("I love to call you 'Sweetheart' " . . . "Because you're very dear, Sweetheart").

Darling: Same as *Sweetheart*, only there are generally fewer of these in most publishers' lines.

Honey: Same as *Sweetheart*, plus some usage for daughters, nieces, and granddaughters. Write some strictly for lovers and some for these relatives (but don't mention "daughter," "niece" or "grand-daughter"). For the latter usage, avoid "I" so that one or more can send.

From Both: Cards sent by married couples or two other related or unrelated people. The recipient may be well-known to one or both. Concentrate on wish-type verses; go easy on compliments and other ideas that suggest closeness. Length: 4 and 8 lines.

Belated Birthday: Cards for Johnny-send-lately's. Some verses offer apologies plus wishes; others stress the positive by saying something on the order of this: "This may be late in coming but the wishes it brings couldn't be warmer" or "Forgot your birthday but couldn't ever forget you." Light or serious. Straightforward or cute. Mostly 4 lines, but some 8 lines. All meters. "I" or no "I."

Teen: These come in two categories: boy and girl. Most are meant to be sent by adults rather than by other teenagers or their juniors. Phrasing has to be fairly unsentimental and straightforward. It's best not to try to pick up on the current vocabulary of teenagers, since the expressions go "in" and "out" so fast. Mostly 4 lines. Some prose, often tied in with the subject of the cover design. Ideas: wishes, compliments (if not too sticky). No "I."

Sixteen (Often *"Sweet Sixteen"*): Almost always for girls. Treatment is usually light, with references to the age and what it means. Compliments, wishes. Mostly 8 lines. No "I." All meters.

Religious: Birthday greeting with a religious message. In some cases the religious content is strong; in others, just a light religious touch is used. Varying degrees of sentiment. Ideas: God bless you, prayer for health and happiness, asking God to care for recipient. The prayer may be combined with general wishes. Biblical quotations may be provided with verses, but this is not necessary; editors usually will apply their own quotations. If you use quotations, give the chapter and verse, and indicate what version of the Bible or what other source you are using. Some verses are aimed specifically at Protestant, Catholic, or Jewish markets; others are made general enough ("God bless you") so that they may be used for people of all religions. Mostly iambic meter. Mostly 8 lines, but some 4. Mostly no "I." Keep in mind that such cards are often sent to people who are ill or infirm.

Service: Most major publishers carry cards specifically meant for men (or women) in the military services. Verses should be tailored to masculine tastes. Not overly sentimental (except for some of the relative Service captions — e.g., Husband, Son and Brother). Don't write all verses in such a way as to suggest that the recipient is overseas or in the field of battle. Ideas: miss you, wishes for luck and happiness, thinking of you, compliments, love (relative captions), comments on how you hope he'll be home again soon. Tone: usually serious, but a light touch is acceptable sometimes. Iambic meter. Length: 4 or 8 lines, some prose.

Illness

General: Most Illness, or Get Well, or Cheer, cards are in the general category, since there are no relative captions and few "special" captions. Cards are written for people of varying degrees of illness — from serious to mild. The relationship of the sender to the recipient may be close or not close. There are many cards in the caption so that there is room for several "I" verses, but most should be sendable by one or more. Tone ranges from light and cheerful to serious and concerned. Meter should be in keeping with tone. Ideas: sorry you're sick (but avoid an overuse of the word "sick," since many editors feel this is too "negative" a word), missing you, thinking of you, compliments ("too nice to be sick"), salutation ("Hello," "Hi and how are you?"), wishes, advice ("Get lots of rest"), and occasionally, love or affection. Length: 4 and 8 lines (as well as 2's and 6's), sometimes longer.

Hospital Illness: Caption often reads: "To You in the Hospital" or "How's the Hospital Patient?" Patient may be hospitalized for many reasons: operation, serious illness, observation, childbirth, convalescence. Don't refer to any of these, because cards ideally must be sendable to all. In some cases you might express the wish that the patient will be home again soon, but don't say this in all verses. Tone: light to serious. Ideas: wishes, mild compliments, thinking of you, "Hello" or "Hi," good-natured advice ("Do everything the doctor says," "Just relax and rest yourself"), reference to hospital. All meters. Length: 4 and 8 lines. Usually no "I."

Accident: In this caption, you are faced with the challenge of writing a verse that is applicable to all kinds of accidents. The recipient may have been hurt in an automobile accident or may have run into a door, but no specific reference can be made. Some verses, by their tone, may suggest a serious accident; others can be written in a less serious vein. Usually no "I."

Operation: Most cards are sent *after* the operation, rather than before, but some are written in such a way that they apply equally well in either case. Don't make reference to specific operations (although some companies publish a card or two for tonsillectomy and appendectomy patients). Tone: light to serious (not all verses should be written on the presumption that the operation was a complete success). Usually no "I." Length: 4 and 8 lines.

Convalescent (or *Cheer* or *Can't Get Well*). This is a fairly large caption group of cards that may be sent to people who either are not expected to recover or are generally infirm. In these cases you can't realistically wish the recipients a return to good health, but you can wish them a nice day, or you can say you're thinking of them. Some "I" and no "I." Both 4 and 8 lines.

Friendship

General: By its very nature, this caption group suggests individual-to-individual communication. "I" verses, therefore, are very much in order. Ideas: value of friendship between sender and recipient, pride, compliments, salutation ("Hello," "Hi"), thinking of you, sometimes wishes. Adjectives play a large part in the balance of this caption group; there are *special* friends, *wonderful* friends, *good* friends, *dear* friends, and just plain friends. Length: 4 and 8 lines, plus some longer ones, especially when inspirational approach is used.

Service: See *Service, Birthday*. Besides General Service, Friendship, there are *As You Enter The Service* and *Love Service* cards.

Sweetheart, Love, Sentimental: These three small captions provide year-round expression of, respectively, sweetheart sentiments ("I" verses), love (most romantic — "I" verses), and warm feelings ("I" or no "I."). Usually 8 lines.

Anniversary

General: This is not a Wedding Anniversary card, although it *may* be used as such. No reference is made to marriage, and the verse is written so that it may be directed to one or more. Cards may be used for all kinds of anniversaries — business, personal, etc. Ideas: wishes, comments on anniversary, maybe memories. No "I." All meters. Length: 4 lines, sometimes 8.

Wedding Anniversary: Cards sent to couples on their anniversary. This is a large category, allowing a wide variety of types: straightforward and lighthearted, sentimental and not, "I" and no "I" (but mostly the latter). Some verses will be written to appeal to those married a short time; others to those married a long time. Ideas: wishes, compliments, memories (the married couple's), sharing, congratulations. Usually there's no reference to family because some couples are childless or no longer have their children living with them, but certainly there should be room for some cards that make mention of "family." All meters. Length: 4, 8 or longer. Some prose, some couplets (2, 4, 6, or 8 lines).

From Both: Wedding anniversary cards sent by two persons, usually a married couple. Same principles apply as in *Wedding Anniversary*, but length is 4 or 8 lines.

Our Own Anniversary: Card is sent by one marriage partner to the other on their anniversary. Verse has to be equally sendable by husband or wife. Range is from semi-sentimental to very sentimental. Tone may be light or serious. Editors keep a balance between verses for young and older couples. Some verses are meant for those very much in love; some, for less enthusiastic lovers. Ideas: love, affection, memories, wishes, compliments, comments on "how much you mean to me," appreciation. Naturally, "I" verses are in order. All meters. Length: 4 or 8 lines, sometimes longer.

Wife Anniversary: Same principles apply as in *Our Own Anniversary*, but cards are specifically intended to be sent by husband to wife.

Husband Anniversary: See *Wife Anniversary*.

First Anniversary: As the name denotes, this card is sent on the first anniversary of a couple's wedding. Reference to this fact should be made in the verse. Light tone seems in order. Length: 4 or 8 lines. No "I."

Mother and Dad, Mother and Father: Cards are sent by children, married or unmarried, to parents on their anniversary. Ideas: wishes, love, memories, pride, compliments, appreciation. No "I." All meters. Length: 4 or 8 lines.

Son and Wife: Cards sent by one or both parents to their son and his wife. Relationship between parents and son (and, more pointedly, between parents and daughter-in-law) may be very close or not so close, so strive for a balance in your verses. Don't write all verses as if the couple has been married a short time. Ideas: love or affection, wishes, compliments, pride. All meters. Length: 4 or 8 lines.

Semi-sentimental to sentimental. Tone: usually serious, sometimes religious. Length: 4 or 8 lines.

Seasonal Captions

Christmas

General: There are many cards in this caption at many prices, so feel free to use several variations. "I" and no "I." Tone: from light to serious. Semi-sentimental to very sentimental. Cards are sent to friends, relatives, neighbors. Ideas: wishes (including, in many cases, wishes for the New Year), compliments, thinking of you, affection, memories, references to imagery of Christmas (trees, snow, Santa, candles, presents, bells, hustle-bustle, etc.). All meters. Length: mostly 4 and 8, but also 2, 6, 12 and 16 lines. Some prose.

Special Captions: See *Birthday* listing for special captions.

Valentine's Day

General: Valentines, which may be sent to friends or relatives, young or old, range from semi-sentimental to very sentimental. Compliments are very much the order of the day, but some verses should be based on other ideas: thinking of you, meaning of day, how much you mean, and general wishes (but avoid wishing "a Happy Valentine's Day," as this is not accepted by many editors). The word *heart* is often used in Valentines, but don't overdo it. All meters. Tone: from light to straightforward. "I" and no "I." Length: 4 and 8 lines, but also 2, 6, 12 and 16. Rarely prose.

Special Captions: See *Birthday* listing for applicable captions.

Easter

General: This is not as big a greeting card occasion as Christmas and Valentine's Day, but still there is a large selection of general Easter cards. Wide range of sentiment. All meters. All lengths. Light to serious in tone. Ideas: wishes (including wishes for "a Happy Spring"), compliments, thinking of you. References to spring are often made.

Special Captions: See *Birthday* listing for applicable captions.

St. Patrick's Day

General: Cards are sent by people Irish and otherwise to people Irish and otherwise. Some verses feature Irish "talk" (*'tis, top o' the mornin', darlin', sure 'n it's a foine day,* etc.), while others are straight "American." Tone is usually light. All meters. Ideas: wishes, compliments, pride of being Irish, thinking of you, meaning of the day (including fun), affection. Semi-sentimental to sentimental. Length: 4 and 8 lines, seldom shorter or longer.

Special Captions: See *Birthday* listings.

Mother's Day

General: Typical captions are: "For You on Mother's Day" and "Happy Mother's Day." Ideas: compliments, honoring recipient on special day, wishes, affection, thinking of you, how much you mean. Tone: light to serious. Semi-sentimental to sentimental. All meters. Length: 4 or 8 lines, sometimes longer.

Relatives: See *Birthday* listing for female relatives. Special emphasis given to *Mother, Mom, Our Mother, Mother from Both,* and *Religious Mother*. There are more cards in these captions offered in the Mother's Day line than in the Everyday line, so there is more latitude in what you may say in your verses — for instance, more "I" verses for *Mother* and *Mom,* more sentiment than usual in some verses, etc. Additional captions in Mother's Day are: *From Your Daughter, From Your Son, From The Kids* (or *From The Family*), *New Mother, Expectant Mother.* In the *Wife* caption, some verses may mention her role as wife and mother, while others should not mention the latter role, since some husbands send their wives Mother's Day cards even though they have had no children.

Father's Day

See Mother's Day. Almost all comments apply to the male counterparts.

Graduation

General: Cards are designed and written to be sent to graduates of all kinds of schools — elementary, junior high, high, college, graduate schools. Tone: light or serious. Ideas: pride (sender's and/or graduate's), wishes, memories of school, compliments. Length: 4 or 8 lines, a few longer. Some prose. Assume in some cases that graduate is continuing his education and in others that he is finished, but avoid specific reference to these factors.

Special Captions: In addition to the captions listed in *General Graduation,* there are cards for the following: *Young Man, Girl, Sweet Girl, Graduate Nurse, As You Enter Profession, Our Wishes, From Both, Sweetheart, Honey, Love, Teacher.*

Thanksgiving

General: Verses are sent to friends and relatives. Semi-sentimental to sentimental. Tone: light or serious. All meters. Ideas: meaning of day, wishes, compliments, warmth or affection, thinking of you, memories. "I" and no "I."

Chapter IV

Conventional Verse: For Example

by Chris FitzGerald

This chapter is a *sample book* of verses that I've sold to various publishers. The verses are intended to serve you as models of what publishers have bought, and as examples of principles of technique, meter, rhyme, level of language, sentiment content, and variations of tone, which were discussed in Chaper II. As you study the verses, note how in many cases the reference to the first person (I or We) is avoided. This is one of the stumbling blocks for new writers.

Although I have tried to give a variety of styles in this chapter, no one writer uses all the many modes of expression that are acceptable in greeting cards, so spend as much time as you possibly can studying published cards. They are your best examples of what greeting card editors are currently buying.

GENERAL BIRTHDAY

Keeping in Touch
With a Birthday Wish
Thank goodness there are birthdays,
Special holidays and such,
If only for the reason
That they help us keep in touch . . .
And that's the thought behind this card
That brings a wish your way
For happiness and heart's content
Today and every day.

(Rust Craft)

GENERAL BIRTHDAY

My Best Wishes
on Your Birthday
I like you
And because I do
I wish to wish
Nice things for you.

> HAPPY BIRTHDAY!
> LOTS OF LUCK!
> LIFE'S BEST ALWAYS!

(Hallmark)

MISCELLANEOUS BIRTHDAY

To Wish a Nice Guy
a Very Happy Birthday

Strictly on the level,
You're a very special guy,
And so it's only fitting
That before this day goes by
You'll get a lot of wishes
Like the one this greeting brings
For a birthday and year just filled
With all your favorite things.

(Hallmark)

DARLING BIRTHDAY

Happy Birthday, Darling

As if I haven't told you so
A thousand times or more,
I love you, Darling, and I hope
Your birthday has in store
A wonderful assortment
Of whatever makes you glad
So you can say this birthday
Was the nicest one you've had.

(Gibson)

BELATED BIRTHDAY

Some People Are
So Forgetful

Look who got forgetful
And who's sorry for it, too
And look who's hoping *every* day
Will be real nice for you —

(Gibson)

WIFE BIRTHDAY

For My Wife
With Love on Your Birthday

I may not always show it,
And I may not always say
The loving things that, really,
You should hear from day to day,
But, Darling, there's no doubt of this —
I think the world of you
And wish you nothing but the best
Today and all year through.
HAPPY BIRTHDAY

(Buzza-Cardozo)

DAUGHTER BIRTHDAY

A Birthday Note of Love
For a Very Dear Daughter

Parents sometimes leave unsaid
The things they ought to say
To make their children more aware
Of how they're loved each day . . .
Well, just in case you're wondering,
This is meant to make it clear
That there's no daughter dearer
Than the girl whose birthday's here.
HOPE YOU HAVE A WONDERFUL DAY
AND A VERY HAPPY YEAR!

(Gibson)

GENERAL ILLNESS

Get Well Soon!

Sincerest wishes
　　set in rhyme
To speed your
　　"getting better" time.

(Gibson)

CAN'T GET WELL

With Sunny Thoughts of You

The nicest thoughts are sunny thoughts,
And that's the very kind
That fills this little greeting
For it's sent with you in mind.

(Gibson)

GENERAL THANK YOU

Appreciate Your Thoughtfulness

You just keep proving all the time
How thoughtful folks can be —
In fact, it's clear that being nice
Is your own specialty.

THANK YOU VERY MUCH

(Charmcraft)

SECRET PAL FRIENDSHIP

"Hi" From Your Secret Pal

To keep you in suspense like this
Is nothing short of shameless
But I don't care 'cause, frankly,
I prefer remaining nameless!

(Gibson)

GENERAL FRIENDSHIP

Hello! Remember Me?

Don't ask me why but I just had
To send a card to you

(Gibson)

To let you know I'm still alive
And just remind you, too
That you are often in my thoughts
Just as you are today
Because your friendship means much more
Than I could ever say.   *(Gibson)*

OUR SYMPATHY

To Express Our Deep Sympathy

Our sympathy is with you
And our hearts are also there,
And may it be a soothing thought
To know how much we care.

(Hallmark)

BOY BABY CONGRATULATIONS — CUTE

A Baby Boy — Hooray for You!

Bet he's full of mischief
And will keep your home supplied
With laughter, fun, excitement,
And a lot of love and pride!

CONGRATULATIONS

(Rust Craft)

WIFE MOTHER'S DAY

For My Wife
on Mother's Day

A world of loving wishes
For the very dearest kind
Of sweetheart, wife and mother
That a man could ever find.

HAPPY MOTHER'S DAY, DEAR

(Paramount)

WEDDING CONGRATULATIONS

A Wish for Your Wedding

To wish you the happiness,
Harmony, love,
And wonderful future
You're both dreaming of!   *(Gibson)*

FROM BOTH WEDDING CONGRATULATIONS

Warmest Wishes From Both of Us
on Your Wedding
Our hearts and wishes go with you
As you begin to live
A life of that sweet happiness
That only love can give.

(Buzza-Cardozo)

WEDDING ANNIVERSARY

With Many Good Wishes
on Your Wedding Anniversary

You must be very happy
As you start another year,
And may it bring you both the things
You hold especially dear,
Including love and laughter,
Best of health for both of you,
And, always, lots of happiness
In everything you do.

(Gibson)

WIFE ANNIVERSARY

For My Wife on Our Anniversary

It's not enough to wish you
"Happy Anniversary," Dear
For there are many other things
That you've a right to hear —
For instance, that you're wonderful,
For instance, that you're sweet,
For instance, that you've done so much
To make my life complete,
And, Dear, you know it's coming
From my heart when I express
My one enduring wish for you —
A wish for happiness.

(Gibson)

Chapter V

Conventional Verse: An Editor's Viewpoint

by Helen Farries

Since conventional verses make up the largest portion of most major greeting card lines, therein lies the greatest opportunity for the free-lance writer. Unfortunately, many writers feel that quantity will bring them more sales than quality, but unless the quality is there, it brings more rejects than acceptances. Most editors, if not all, are on budgets, usually smaller lately than we'd like to have, so we're becoming more choosey than in the past. We can't just buy, we have to have a place to use the sentiments. In addition, we have people who decide whether the verses we're offering for the particular cards are accepted. They decide on the ones I write in the same way. Inasmuch as there are many more people writing greeting verses than ever before and many more good writers submitting, the competition is much greater. Editors now have to be more selective. All you'd need to do would be to see the quantity of mail we get every day to realize this.

Today's sentiments on cards are slanted toward the natural or normal conversation more than they used to be. They can have a light touch, may be long or short, prose or rhyme — so long as the sentiment is in keeping with the title and the occasion. We want good writing more than ever before. Meter and readability are stressed.

Having been a free-lance writer myself for a number of years before becoming an editor, I can appreciate the free-lance writer's feelings and viewpoint as well as the editor's. I know the joy of selling and the disappointment of rejections. I know the thrill of seeing my work in a beautiful card, and still remember the first finished card I ever saw with a verse of mine in it; so I know yours, too. In fact, I still feel that way when I see one of mine that I feel is exceptionally good and well done. I still remember my first check, and I always smile when a writer thanks me for a check that meant a first sale — and says, "I feel like framing it and keeping it." I felt that way, too, about mine.

As a free-lance writer, I was considered rather successful, and there were some things that I feel contributed to that success, which are as valid today as then. I know, as an editor, they would make my work easier and more enjoyable, if I saw them in the ideas writers submit to me, so I'll pass them along to you.

Since editors have such a quantity of ideas and verses to choose from these days, and can buy only so many, I'd suggest that you try something I found very satisfactory.

Select a number of companies you'd like to write for . . . six . . . eight, ten! Write about ten or twelve verses for each one — no more at one time — and send them out to the respective editors. If you have this many working for you all the time and write acceptable and good material, some of them will bring the good news you're hoping for and that check you desire. As each group comes back, replace anything that was bought with another new verse and send them along to the next editor on the list until you've made the rounds. Don't be dejected by rejections. Remember, we're not all looking for the same thing at the same time, and even though your sentiments are good, if we cannot use them immediately,

we often cannot take them . . . and sometimes what you feel
is really good may not fit into our needs or lines.

I followed this method religiously for several years, and I
received a check almost every day, and sometimes two or three.
They weren't always big checks, but they all added up. Working
this way, I didn't have to worry frantically about hearing immediately from each editor to see if my verses were being accepted.
It was easier on the editor and on me, too, and believe me, I
know how much work an editor has who is conscientious, as
I try to be, and who reads every sentiment that comes in, as I
do, and sincerely tries to help the free-lance writer. Most editors
are that way.

Become acquainted with the lines you're writing for. Remember that the editors have their styles and preferences and
that what they like is usually reflected in the sentiments.
While all good material, particularly the conventional, is
similar, there's a trend or a feeling that gives you an idea
as to what might be chosen . . . if you're familiar with the
lines.

I researched all lines, when I was free-lancing, and I still do,
for it's necessary to keep up with the competition, to know the
changes, the new things, the good things that are your competition. It helps you to see what verses were accepted and gives
you an idea of what kind to write that might have a chance to
be accepted, too.

Be appreciative of the editor's suggestions and criticisms . . .
and appreciative of the time it takes to offer both. It usually
means that you have possibilities if you'll change things a
little or be a little more aware of what's needed, and what's
wrong.

I was very fortunate, for I had two wonderfully kind editors,
who certainly gave me time that I know now was very precious,

and whose criticism and suggestions, I'm certain, were great factors in my success then as well as now. In fact, there is one to whom I feel the credit goes for my becoming the editor I wanted to be when I was free-lancing. She's still an editor of one of the leading greeting card companies, a highly successful one, and a most wonderful person: Helen Steiner Rice, of Gibson Greeting Cards.

Don't deluge an editor with many verses at one time. Psychologically, it's upsetting, and good as they may be, the editor may return many more than might be considered otherwise. Let a week or so elapse between groups. There's always time for more as editors usually work on their lines for several weeks, and there are too many sentiments coming in every week to hold many of everyone's. What has to be returned one week may be needed in another week or two. If you're a good writer, and the material is needed, the editor will try hard to place your work and will advise you of the needs in plenty of time.

Subscribe to a good writer's magazine like Writer's Digest . . . There's frequently good information in them about greeting card needs, and even the non-greeting card material may help you and even give you leads to other writing that you may do successfully. I read every writing magazine there is because I often find helpful hints about writing. They also help me to know what is going on in other writing fields, and what other greeting card editors are buying and paying. That way I can suggest writers try there, if their needs are different from ours at the time.

Now, let's talk about specific conventional verses, and let's start out with how to be conventional in an unconventional way.

A verse like *Wishing You Every Blessing at this Joyous Season* is an excellent sentiment, but it is something editors don't buy because it's too easily written and we can use the money for something we need more. But here is a sentiment I did buy because the writer made it a little different: *May Joy Surround You This Christmas Like a Wreath of Blessings.* It was a new slant and a lovely one, and the writer deserved the check I sent her.

Another sentiment that was a little different and that earned a check was : *Wishing you a really Once-Upon-A-Time Christmas.* It expressed a nostalgic feeling in a new and whimsical way.

Sometimes it's just the tone of a verse, nothing so unusual in what it's saying but the way it's said that sells it. For example:

> Some wishes are friendly,
> Some wishes are gay,
> Some wishes are loving
> And this one's that way . . .
> Because it's for someone
> Who's specially dear
> And nice to remember
> When Christmas is here.

This gives you a happy, warm feeling just to read it; so you know it will give the buyer of the card and the receiver the same feeling.

A birthday verse that had a happy lilt and brought a well-deserved check to the writer was this one:

> Gather a handful of roses,
> Some sunbeams, a rainbow or two,
> A couple of stars to wish on
> To bring all your special dreams true,
> Tie them with ribbons of memories,
> The kind that are lovely and sweet,
> And have the kind of a birthday
> You'd love to repeat and repeat!

This is a little poetic but that adds to its charm and warmth.

Another with that same kind of feeling, but short, that I found in a free-lance writer's group and bought:

BE HAPPY ON YOUR BIRTHDAY

Hope the sky's as blue
As a bluebird's wings,
And the day's just filled
With wonderful things!

Another more conventional perhaps, but with a little different rhyme pattern brought a check to the writer. It was this:

ON YOUR BIRTHDAY

Don't count the years,
That's not the issue . . .
Just count your friends
And the joys they wish you!

It's short, sincere, warm, and complimentary with its mention of your many friends and their wishes for you.

Wedding and anniversary sentiments may be varied in many ways, too. Besides those for Mother and Dad, Sister and Husband, Son and Wife, Golden and Silver and such special titles, here are some that interested me:

HAPPY ANNIVERSARY

It's obvious you two have found . . .
It's love that makes the world go 'round!

The design was light, of course, and it compliments the couple subtly on their happy life together.

Another that says a lot in a few words and is truly complimentary and warm and conversational:

So glad you found each other . . .
You're perfect together!

Now, this isn't saying the longer general or sentimental anniversary verses aren't popular. They still are and we use many of them. When you take the sentiment out of greeting cards, you take the joy out of them.

Here's a sentimental Wedding verse that got the committee's approval. You'll notice there's an old proverb setting the theme. Naturally you'd expect the design to have roses on it, and it did!

TIME BRINGS ROSES

May time fulfill the happy dreams
You two are sharing now,
Make dearer still the words you say
As you repeat your vow,
May time bring sweeter memories,
As it goes on its way,
And may the love and joy you share
Grow deeper every day.

The short, formal sentiment which we use but don't pay for because it's too easy to write is: *Wishing you every happiness in your life together.* However, here's one a little different. It, too, is built around an old saying that will be familiar to you:

HAPPINESS SEEMS MADE TO BE SHARED

Somebody wrote that long ago . . .
May you two always find it so.

Variety, we've all heard, is the spice of life, so we need all kinds of sentiments in all categories.

Convalescent and Cheer cards need much variety and there are many of them in most of our lines. The Cheer card is almost like, and often used as, a friendship card. They are used for shut-ins and for persons where you don't want to mention their condition. Here's one that has been in our line for many, many years and still sells as well as ever:

WITH CHEERY THOUGHTS

I've tucked a lot of cheery thoughts
In with this card for you . . .

> Just wish that it was big enough
> To bring me with it, too.

A convalescent sentiment that brought a well-deserved check was this:

WONDERING HOW YOU'RE FEELING

> Although I can't drop in today,
> Of this I can assure you,
> This little card brings thoughts enough
> And love enough to cure you!

Another that sent a check to the free-lance writer was this:

SO SORRY YOU'RE SICK . . .

> But for every single minute
> That you have to spend in bed,
> May there be hours of sunshine
> And perfect health ahead!

Another cheer card that won the committee's approval and made a sale for the writer was:

THINKING OF YOU SO MUCH

> I think of you often,
> But you'll never know it,
> Unless I get busy
> And send this to show it!

This could be used as a friendship card, too. Most cheer cards can be used both ways.

Remember, all convalescent and cheer cards are not short. We use many longer ones. We use many titles, too, like *Hospital* and *Welcome Home from the Hospital, Operation, Accident, Our Wishes, From All of Us, Masculine* sentiments, etc.

The *Friendship* lines are large ones, too, and need much variety. Here's a short one I bought:

JUST HAD A LOVELY THOUGHT . . . YOU!

Another I bought and that has been used in *Friendship, Birthday* and *Seasonal* lines:

JUST THINKING . . .
> The world is filled
> With all too few
> Wonderful people
> Like YOU!

And another:

YOU'RE THE NICEST FRIEND
> Friendship like yours
> Is something dear . . .
> Something to treasure
> Year after year.

Again, there are as many kinds of friendship verses as there are convalescents, including many titles. There's the *Just to Say Hello* card, the *Missing You,* the *Thinking of You,* the *Special Friend* and endless others. Here's a short one I found in a contributor's group one day and bought:

HELLO
> Just thinking of you . . .
> And the day's well spent
> When I think of you,
> If there's not another thing I do!

And a longer *Hello* sentiment that I bought from a free-lance writer:

JUST SAYING HELLO
> There's always a reason
> For thinking of you
> And taking a minute
> To tell you so, too;
> For you're someone special
> And so nice to know

It's always a pleasure
Just saying HELLO!

Another one that's the *Missing You* type which brought a check:

WISHING WE WERE TOGETHER TODAY

When I feel lonely
Or when I'm blue,
My thoughts just naturally
Turn to YOU,
For you are always
So cheerful and gay,
Just the thought of you
Can brighten my day!

One of the *Thinking of You* type that brought a check:

THINK OF YOU SO MUCH

Though I don't write very often,
I've not forgotten you,
But busy days are keeping me
From all I'd like to do!
Would love to hear your voice again
And see your cheery smile . . .
I think of you so many times,
Not just once-in-awhile!

That is a little different version of the *Missing You* type. Others are lighter and shorter and they're popular, too.

Thank You cards? There never seem to be enough of those in anyone's line. There are all lengths of verse, all degrees of warmth and formality. The special titles in *Thank You* cards are *To All of You, From All of Us, In Appreciation, For Hospitality, For Gifts,* and the *Thank You* that covers anything without saying what! Here's one of those that I bought that is very popular:

Are you just nice naturally
Or just naturally nice?

This might easily be used as a friendship card, too, as might this popular one in our line:

Nice people do nice things

Both compliment the receiver for whatever the gratefulness is for. They say a lot in a few words!

Two other examples of warm *Thank You* verses that cover many situations are these:

WITH MORE THANKS THAN WORDS CAN SAY

How do you thank a person like you?
There just isn't any way!
You're always doing some lovely thing
To brighten someone's day!

Or this one:

WE CAN'T THANK YOU ENOUGH

If you're as nice to everyone,
We've just one thing to say —
You surely must get cards like this
A dozen times a day!

These sentiments cover any situation you want to use them for — a gift, a visit, a little kindness.

Besides the usual birth congratulations, which we surely need and use, here are two that have a little different slant:

LOVE TO YOU AND THAT SWEET NEW BABY

A baby's like a flower,
All soft and pink and white,
A baby's like a sunbeam,
All sparkly, warm and bright,
A baby's like a bluebird
That brings a happy song,
And life is so much sweeter
When a baby comes along!

The title carries your greeting and the verse is one of the more sentimental, poetic type.

The other one just says: *Hear you have the cutest little thing a stork could bring! Congratulations and Best Wishes.*

Don't forget the new *Grandparents,* those with a First baby, those with twins, those whose baby was a boy, those who had a girl. We use verses in all these titles.

The *Sympathy* line uses many conventional sentiments. They range from the strictly formal, which we rarely buy, to the prose, which we buy only when it is something a little out of the usual, to the general and warmer type of verse. Here's a prose we bought because it was expressed in a different and lovely way:

> Let the memory of a beautiful life
> bring fresh hope to your sorrowing heart.

Here's an example of a longer sentiment expressing warmth, but not too sentimentally worded:

> There are no words to let you know
> The sympathy this brings,
> It seems somewhat at times like this,
> Words are such empty things,
> But many are the thoughts and prayers
> These two words bring your way,
> Just these two words, "With Sympathy"
> So deeply felt today.

There are many religious and inspirational sympathy sentiments, of course. There are also special titles like *With Sympathy in the Loss of a Mother* or *of a Father, From Both of Us,* and *With Our Sympathy.*

While we have mentioned a few birthday verses, we make a large line of them: short, long, warm, intimate, prose, rhyme, light, serious, relative, special friend, You'll always be Young,

The Boss, Across the Miles, Secret Pal, Mutual, From Both of Us, All of Us. All of these titles are in the seasonal lines, too. I'll give a few examples that show broad range of styles and titles that won the committee's approval. Here is a *Special Friend's Birthday* verse:

> It's the little things you do
> That bring pleasure day by day,
> Your friendly smiles, your handclasp
> In that "glad-to-know-you" way,
> It's the way you understand
> And know just what to do . . .
> Who wouldn't love and treasure
> A perfect friend like YOU!

Of course, it has the usual *Happy Birthday* title. *Special Friend* cards are very popular and are usually sent from woman to woman; hence, are usually warm, even when light.

Since *Grandmothers* are usually favorites, their verses are usually warm and sentimental. Here's one of that kind:

> Thinking of the little things
> You do in your sweet way,
> Loving things that make it seem
> Like Christmas every day,
> And wishing you the blessings,
> The joy and gladness, too
> That you deserve, Grandmother
> For all these things you do!

Mother and *Mom* are favorite titles, too, and their verses are usually warm and loving, though often light. Here's an example of a sentimental prose for *Mother's* birthday:

> Mother, you never change —
> except to keep on growing dearer and more wonderful.
> Love on Your Special Day

Now, let's examine one for *Mother's Birthday,* which we also use for *Daughter, Sister, Grandma, Husband* — and for all seasons.

> The nice things you do
> Mean more than you know
> And this is the day
> For telling you so,
> And surely the day
> For telling you, too
> How nice it is having
> A Mother like YOU!

This avoids the "I" or "We" thus giving it a wide usage, yet it is warm. It is loving without being overly so. It is conversational.

Here's a *Mom* verse I bought:

> As I grow older, Mom,
>   I see
> How many things you did
>   for me,
> And now, with all my love,
>   I say —
> Thanks, Mom, and have a
>   happy day!

A light one for sister, which brought a check, though it's a very simple verse:

> Just Between Us, Sister . . .
> This wish is special . . .
> because YOU are!

Another for sister that's more sentimental, which has also been used for *Mother, Aunt, Grandma, Mom* is this one:

> "Sweet" sounds a little
> Sentimental I guess,
> But that's what you are . . .
> With a CAPITAL "S!"

A lovely prose verse for a *Mother and Dad Christmas* title was this one:

> No Christmas memory
> would be half as dear . . .
> if it didn't include you two!

Of course, we use many longer, sentimental verses for Mother and Dad. Here's another short but nice one:

> If love could come in packages
> All wrapped up bright and gay,
> We know who'd get a stack of them
> This happy Christmas Day!

Some *Darling, Wife, and Sweetheart* cards get really sentimental. Here's one to *My Wife* that I bought:

> I love sharing Christmas
> The way we do, Dear,
> I love being with you
> To start the New Year,
> I love you for doing
> The sweet things you do
> That make me so thankful
> I share life with YOU!

This could be for *Husband,* too, of course, by leaving the word *Wife* out of the sentiment. That's something to remember, it gives your sentiment a broader usage.

Now, here's one for *Sweetheart.* The title sets the theme. Sub-titles are eye catchers for editors as well as people looking for a card to buy.

> Merry Christmas, Sweetheart . . .
> "Why do I love Christmas?"

> WHY DO I LOVE CHRISTMAS?
> It isn't just the candles
> With all their sparkly glow,

It isn't just the carols,
The bells and mistletoe . . .
It's true, all these make Christmas
A time of joy and cheer,
They all add to the gladness
Around this time of year!
But more than all these, Sweetheart,
And more than all else, too,
Christmas is a time I love
Because of loving YOU!

Seasons, especially *Christmas* and *Easter,* have many special things to talk about that let you work on the imagination more. It makes them fun to write and nice to read by both the sender and receiver. This one is sentimental but much shorter:

All my love and a Merry Christmas
to the one who makes every day a happy one for me.

You couldn't ask much more than that of anyone, now could you? Being the sentimental type myself, I'd really prefer getting the longer one, and I usually get that kind, too, from my husband.

Darling verses are usually written so they may be used for husbands and wives, although it isn't mentioned in the sentiment.

It doesn't take carols,
It doesn't take bells,
It doesn't take candles and trees,
It doesn't take holly,
It doesn't take pine,
Though Christmas is made up of these,
It only takes sharing,
It only takes love,
For these are the things that bring cheer . . .
I have YOU to SHARE THEM,
I have YOU to LOVE . . .
I have everything I hold dear!

The writer lets all the things we love about Christmas set the theme, giving a nostalgic feeling to the sender and receiver. This card tells the receiver the way you feel with lots of love and sentiment! You could say almost the same thing in one like this:

> Merry Christmas with All My Love
> to the one who means everything to me.

We need those, too, for that's all some people want to say, and we have to please all people.

That should be examples enough. You should by now have the idea it takes both long and short, both rhyme and prose, both *very* sentimental and not so sentimental, light and serious to please all persons — and all editors. It's much harder to pack a lot of feeling into four lines than into eight or twelve, but both are needed, and if you have something in that longer verse that makes it stand out, there's usually a place for it sooner or later. We may have to ask you to return it later, but you will usually find it will sell eventually.

I've tried to show you a variety of verses that "made it," and I've tried to show you why they did. I've tried to show you the depth and breadth of the conventional lines and the ways you can be conventional in an unconventional way at times. I hope I have shown you how many titles there are, although there are many more than I've mentioned, and there are more every year.

I do want to make a few additional suggestions. I receive many verses that just seem to rhyme and have little feeling or meaning. Now, such verses bring no joy — and few checks. No one is more conscious of how hard it is sometimes to find rhyming words than I, even when you use rhyming dictionaries, but it's better to think about an idea and change it around so that it sounds natural. If your card sits on the counter unsold, no one will be happy. Such care takes a little more time and you may not write quite as many, but your chances for selling are better. Remember, quality sells more verses than quantity. Another thing to watch: don't use unnatural rhymes, or words in unusual order like —

> I wish you joy on Christmas Day
> And may it with you always stay!

You'd never say that to anyone and so of course we'd never buy it! Things like that are sometimes done in poetry. They call it poetic license, I believe; but ours is a personal message and it's conversational, and we don't do it!

Don't try to be *too* different. Many people try so hard to be different that you feel it. Just try to give your sentiments that little extra something, that little unconventional twist, that sells them.

When you're sending such titles as *Why Don't You Write? — I'll Write — Secret Pal, Across the Miles, Belated Anniversary, Twins Birthday* or *Birth Congratulations* for twins or first baby, *Retirement,* etc., don't send six of one title only. Since most companies use few of these titles, all or most of them will bring a rejection slip. Include them by all means, but with others like *birthdays, anniversaries, friendship,* and *get wells* that are more likely to be needed. Every title is important, but some are much more limited merely because the card companies use fewer of them.

Sub-titles are eye catchers, so think about them. For example, *Happy Birthday, Sister,* with sub-title: *Remembering Happy Times with You; On Valentine's Day, Sweetheart,* with sub-title: *Because You're All the Things I Love;* or *Happy Birthday, Dad,* with sub-title: *Thanks for Being So Wonderful.* These immediately set up a favorable reaction and make the buyer look inside. They catch the attention of the editors, too. We have to be aware of what the buyers will like.

While things have changed a bit since I was a free-lance writer, many things are the same or similar. We still have some of the verses in our line that I sold as a free-lance writer. Here's a get well example for which I was paid $2.00 many years ago: *If your friends don't get you out of here . . . your enemas will!* It is still designed as I suggested in words, — I cannot draw — and obviously is a card for the *Hospital* patient. This is a humorous card; when I was a free-lance writer, I wrote all types of cards. In fact, after I became editor, I wrote over 90% of the entire Buzza-Cardozo line for more than fifteen years. We were, of course, much smaller then.

I've written all my life, sold my first jingle at ten. For years I wrote verses for friends and relatives, as many of you have done, but didn't try selling anything until much later. I had my heart set on being the editor of Buzza-Cardozo and worked toward it from the start. As I mentioned before, I had much help from editors, and am deeply appreciative of it. I had great respect and appreciation for their suggestions and help, which I tried to show, in the quality of my work. As a result, I was rewarded with the dream of my heart coming true.

We can't all be editors for there aren't that many card companies. We can't all even be staff writers, for even these are too few for the many writers who free-lance. But the opportunity to write and to express our thoughts and feelings in words is open to all who wish to try, and for those who have the talent and ability, there is a chance for doing the thing that you love — to write and sell and fulfill that something in you that seems to be in most writer's hearts.

Just remember — I *know* — *quality brings far greater rewards than quantity . . . sincerity is the surest secret of success.* — Words aren't enough. No matter how beautifully written, they must have meaning. There's not a fortune for most people in free-lance writing, but there's great joy in making others happy, in giving comfort and hope, expressing love and friendship, appreciation and good wishes with your words and thoughts. And there's greater success than you might dream for those who have talent and who use it wisely and well to make greeting cards the wonderful means of communication, and the wonderful way to express happiness, love, friendship, gratefulness and sympathy they are today!

Words aren't magic by themselves. You put the magic in them. Success is possible, but it has to be worked for, unless you are a genius — and few are. It has always been my theory that life gives us two answers, Yes or No. You may get No, even if you try, but you're sure to get it if you don't, and there's always a chance for Yes if you have the ability and try hard enough.

I haven't given you many poor examples of verses because I think the good ones give you a better idea of what I like, and I'm sure other editors do, too. Hopefully, the verses I've given you will stimulate you to write new and better ones to submit to us. Greeting card editors are always looking for something good, something lovely, something new.

Chapter VI

The Inspirational Verse

by Helen Farries

The inspirational verse 'per se' has only been 'labeled' as such in the past few years, when it has really come into its own.

I began this type of verse in the Buzzo-Cardozo lines in 1954, although we didn't 'label it' as such until several years later. Now, almost every major company has a line of inspirational cards.

According to one dictionary definition, inspirational means "produced by or moved by inspiring," and that is the purpose of the sentiments: to inspire, to lift, to give hope, assurance, faith, and love. Everyone seeks, needs and searches for these things, especially in today's world.

There are many reasons why inspirational cards are popular. They cover many needs, occasions, and situations; they embody all religions and convey deep feeling and concern, lovely thoughts and sincere affection; and they have a deeper meaning than the average conventional sentiment.

Inspirationals are usually scheduled with the religious lines, although they are not always strictly religious in language. They may or may not mention God. They may or may not use Bible texts. They often are inspired by old proverbs and familiar writings of persons like Emerson, Jeremy Taylor, Dryden, Tennyson and Shakespeare. I just finished writing one I'm submitting for approval next week. I used a lovely quote from Tennyson — 'What Shall I Give?' — as both the title and the theme of the sentiment. I wish I could tell you about it, but I don't know yet if our committee (who votes on my verses just as they do yours) will accept it. If they do, then maybe someday you'll see it in the card stores.

Here is a birthday card, inspirational, that I did some time ago that we have had a request to have returned to the line. This time, the quote is mine, and is used as a motto title. Naturally, the card is designed with a border of flowers making a setting for the message. The words and the designs are very closely related in the good inspirational card. The title reads:

Life's
Like a Lovely
Garden,
With Memories
as
Flowers,
And
God Gives Us the
Privilege
To Choose What Goes
in Ours.

On the left page inside, it says Happy Birthday to You, and on the right, there is this sentiment:

> You've planted LOVE and FRIENDSHIP,
> And since you planted these,
> Your Garden's surely BLOOMING
> With LOVELY memories . . .
> And life has been much brighter
> For EVERYONE you've known
> Because of all the GLADNESS
> And HAPPINESS you've sown!

You'll notice the only mention of God is in the motto title in this verse, but it plays an important part in the message.

Another, in which I quote from Shakespeare for the title is:

A YEAR? A LIFE? ... WHAT ARE THEY?

We count our birthdays by the years,
And with each one we add,
We count them short, if they've brought joy,
And long, if they've been sad,
But count the years the way we will,
For all hold joys and tears,
Life is God's glorious gift to us
Of rich and happy years!

You can see how the quote inspired this type of sentiment.

A little one that has no quote, no Bible text, and no mention of God, but that is definitely inspirational is this one, a motto type, as many inspirationals are:

The sun is always shining
somewhere . . .
Just because you cannot see it,
Doesn't prove it isn't there.

Of course, it carries the simple prose greeting inside — *With Love.* There's plenty of room for your own personal message. We did a series of these and they were well received. All of them were motto type titles with simple prose sentiments inside like *Thinking of You, Keep Faith, Have a Happy Day,* etc. The designs were very important in these. In fact, many persons told us they kept them and framed them.

Love is something all writers like to write about and surely a good theme for inspirations. Here is a beautiful sentiment, a motto type title and a powerful one. The cover said:

What is it but LOVE
That can sweeten a flower,
Or send a bright rainbow
To follow a shower . . .
That can carve out a mountain,
Give wings to a dove,
And bring our hearts comfort . . .
What is it but LOVE?

(inside)
LOVE is as old as the heavens are high,
LOVE is as real as the stars in the sky,
LOVE is the motive for sharing and giving,
LOVE is the one thing that makes life worth living,
LOVE is the PRESENCE of GOD shining through . . .
LOVE is the reason I send this to YOU!

This is the type of sentiment that fits the Valentine line as well as the Everyday Friendship line.

Another motto title on Love that has been very popular in our line fits the Valentine Line as well as the Everyday Friendship Line. The cover reads:

JUST A LITTLE MORE LOVE
There's a gift we can give
Every day that we live,
Which we all have an endless share of,
There's a way we can bless
And bring more happiness,
All it is . . . JUST A LITTLE MORE LOVE!

(Inside)
It can be in a prayer
Or some moment we share
Or a message like this one today . . .
JUST A LITTLE MORE LOVE,
Which we've all plenty of,
And which grows when we give it away!
When it's given, we've learned,
It's not only returned,
But it makes earth like heaven above . . .
So I send on its way
My heart's gift for the day . . .
All it is . . . JUST A LITTLE MORE LOVE!

An unusual format gives this Easter Inspirational an interesting appeal. The sentiment is written in the shape of a cross:

> Trusting the
> Eternal
> Promise,
> "Behold, I
> make all
> things new" . . .
> Seeing it in every blossom,
> Every new leaf sprouting, too,
> Finding it in all around us,
> If we'll only look and see . . .
> For us all
> There are
> New blessings,
> There's
> Fresh hope
> Eternally

With competition what it is today, it helps to use your originality. The same thing is often done with a Christmas tree or bell.

Here's another example of a very popular one with us, which uses a Bible text as the title:

> Faith is the substance of things hoped for,
> the evidence of things not seen. — Hebrews 11:1
>
> Who sees the rosebud in the seed
> That's dropped into the ground?
> Who sees the love that we are told
> Makes this world go around?
> Who sees beyond this day — this hour
> What's on ahead — but those
> Who have the FAITH to plant the seed
> And KNOW there'll be a rose!

Many times the inspirational just plants the *thought,* as that one does. It's always an *assuring* thought. The verse you just read gives the assurance of what faith can do. Here's a popular one with only a few words, which gives the assurance of what love can do:

Sometimes a little touch of love
That we know someone feels,
Not only brightens up a day . . .
It blesses and it heals.

A short prose inside assures the receiver of your love and adds the hope that it will comfort and bless the receiver.

The first inspirational I ever wrote is still the best selling card in our line. It has been in the line continuously since 1954. We get more letters about it than about any other card. Used for many occasions, we are told, it is often bought six or more at a time by persons who like to have the card on hand. It has been recorded twice on inspirational albums, once by Mahalia Jackson in her great album, *Mahalia,* where she sings it with great feeling. It has been used in the seasonal lines as well as the Everyday Friendship Line.

I THOUGHT OF YOU AND SAID A LITTLE PRAYER

This morning when I wakened
And saw the sun above,
I softly said, "Good Morning, Lord,
Bless everyone I love!"

Right away I thought of you
And said a little prayer
That He would bless you specially
And keep you free from care . . .

I thought of all the happiness
A day could hold in store,
And wished it all for you because
No one deserves it more!

I felt so warm and good inside,
My heart was all aglow . . .
I know God heard my prayer for you,
He hears them all you know!

This is a very simple sentiment, but a very sincere one. Perhaps that's part of its success and appeal. At any rate, it's a great joy to me to know, no matter how the day has gone, that hundreds have been blessed, given joy, hope, and assurance through these simple words of mine. I got the inspiration for this verse from a friend's little daughter. She came home from school and told us a minister had told a joke in chapel that day. He said some people wake up and say, *Good Lord, it's morning!* Others wake up and say, *Good morning, Lord!*

Another we published that year, which is still in our lines, and which receives its share of grateful letters from receivers and senders alike is this one:

THE MAGIC OF PRAYER

When the trials of this life make you weary
And your troubles seem too much to bear,
There's a wonderful solace and comfort
In the silent communion of prayer.

When you've searched for the sun without ceasing
And the showers continue to fall,
There's a heavenly lift in this wonderful gift
That God has extended to all.

For the magic of prayer there comes power
That will minimize all of your care,
And you'll gather new hope when you're able to cope
With the troubles that once brought despair.

So lift up your heart to the heavens,
There's a loving and kind Father there,
Who offers release and comfort and peace
In the silent communion of prayer.

That is a powerful verse. I bought it from a free-lance writer. I met her several years later and could understand why she wrote such a beautiful sentiment; she herself is a warm and beautiful person.

That same year we published two other verses entitled: "The Magic of Love" and "The Magic of Christmas," which are both still in our line. "The Magic of Love" is in the Wedding Line, but has been in the Friendship Line and the Valentine Line with a different ending. With still another ending, it has been used and recorded as an inspirational song. It, too, has received many letters of appreciation and praise. I always feel when total strangers take the time to write letters about certain sentiments they like, it is a sign that we've been successful in giving the world something worthwhile. That's really much of the joy of writing and of being an editor, and I think the inspirational sentiments offer that kind of joy more than any other type of sentiment.

What makes verses like the two sentiments we have just read popular year after year? Inspirationals are timeless — more so than other sentiments. Those who love them want to use them over and over. Those who have been comforted and blessed by them treasure and want to send them to others.

There's always room for new ideas, too. Here's the Wedding version of the "Magic of Love":

> There's a wonderful gift that can give you a lift,
> It's a blessing from heaven above!
> It can comfort and bless, it can bring happiness —
> It's the wonderful MAGIC OF LOVE!
>
> Like a star in the night, it can keep your faith bright,
> Like the sun, it can warm your hearts, too —
> It's a gift you can give every day that you live,
> And when given, it comes back to you!
>
> When love lights the way, there is joy in the day
> And all troubles are lighter to bear,
> Love is gentle and kind, and through love you will find
> There's an answer to your every prayer!
>
> May it never depart from your two loving hearts,
> May you treasure this gift from above —
> You will find if you do, all your dreams will come true,
> In the wonderful MAGIC OF LOVE!

Now, the "Magic of Christmas":

> It's in the carols sweet and clear,
> It's in the churchbells that you hear,
> It's far away and it is near . . .
>
> ### IT'S EVERYWHERE!
>
> It's in the sun and in the snow,
> It's in the candles all aglow,
> It's underneath the mistletoe . . .
>
> ### IT'S IN EACH PRAYER!
>
> It's in the trees and in the toys,
> It's in the happy girls and boys,
> It's in the memories and the joys . . .
>
> ### IT'S SET APART!
>
> It's in the Shepherds on the Hill,
> It's in the words, 'Peace and Good Will,'
> It's in the quiet and the still . . .
>
> ### IT'S IN THE HEART!

Of course, we add the wish Merry Christmas to give it a greeting. The word *magic,* in both of these, and the one mentioned earlier, "The Magic of Prayer," intrigue the buyer into seeing what that magic is. The sentiments make it clear, and since it's a magic we all, or most of us, recognize and believe in, many sales are assured.

Inspirationals are very popular in Sympathy cards. In sorrow, everyone needs to be comforted, assured of love, understanding, help, and hope. It's hard for us to voice these things, and the inspirational verse does it for us in a beautiful way. Here are a few examples of popular ones with us. This one uses a Bible text as its title:

THROUGH FAITH WE UNDERSTAND . . . Hebrews 11:3

> Faith tells us there'll be a tomorrow
>   After today is gone,
> The sun will shine and the wind will blow,
>   As time goes on and on!

Faith tells us the flowers will blossom,
    It tells us there'll be rain,
We've seen the evidence of these things
    Again, again and again!
So how can we doubt that love lives on,
    If all these things are true?
God bless the prayers this brings today,
    God bless and comfort you.

Here's another that we receive many letters about from people who have sent it and from those who have received it. We've had to keep it in the line, because of continued requests.

THERE MUST BE A REASON WE CAN'T SEE

There must be a reason we can't see,
There must be a reason why,
A reason that we must take 'on Faith,'
As we do the sun on high . . .
There must be an answer why it is
That one who enjoyed life so,
Why someone who is so dear to us,
    Suddenly has to go.

Life is a journey, so we are told,
For some, long . . . others, brief,
A journey on which we all find joy
Mingled with sadness and grief . . .
Try to remember the joy today,
    However hard it may be,
And trust you'll find comfort when you know
    The reason you now can't see.

I'm sure everyone has asked that question: Why did it have to happen to her or to him? This seems to help to answer it, or at least, to offer comfort, by the many letters we have received.

The next one is not the usual type of Sympathy sentiment or title, but it seems to have quite an appeal. Both the title and sentiment do what an inspirational card should do. They give assurance of being loved and needed and convey the feeling that someone understands and perhaps has been through a similar sorrow or experience. You know there are other sorrows besides losing a loved one, very great sorrows. This sentiment seems to cover both kinds of sorrow.

THERE'S SOMEONE WHO LOVES YOU AND NEEDS YOU

> To be loved and needed
> When we're needing love
> Sometimes brings the comfort
> We're so in need of,
> And often it helps us
> When we're feeling blue
> To comfort another
> Who needs our love, too.

You'll notice that we include ourselves in the thought so that we do not seem to be 'preaching'. The verse intimates that we understand and that we too have, perhaps, experienced a sorrow of this kind.

Now, let's take a look at an inspirational Convalescent. The title uses an old proverb:

PATIENCE IS A FLOWER THAT GROWS NOT IN EVERYONE'S GARDEN

> It takes a while for flowers to bloom
>   After we plant the seeds,
> We have to give them loving care,
>   Like every flower needs . . .
> They don't just 'push up through the sod'
>   And blossom over night,
> But when they do burst through in bloom,
>   They make a lovely sight!
> Sometimes it's that way with us, too,
>   Some things take time, we find,
> So just be patient and keep faith
>   Till this is all behind!

Again, we include ourselves in this thought. It seems to make the sentiment a little 'closer' and gives assurance that time, faith, and loving care are great healers.

Some Inspirational Friendship sentiments do not use Bible texts, do not have any religious words, yet surely imply them.

A NEW DAY BEGINS THIS MORNING

Yesterday's in the past now,
With all that 'might have been,
Never to be lived over,
Never to be seen again!
Tomorrow's in the future,
And none of us can see
What tomorrow holds in store,
But what will be . . . will be!
But today the world's made new,
What's in it . . . who can say?
But we've a fresh beginning . . .
So let's enjoy TODAY!

Both title and the sentiment give a hopeful feeling. There is no Bible text in either the title or verse, but doesn't it remind you of the text, "Behold, I make all things new?"

This one has as its title the one word *Hope,* beautifully designed, to make it more effective.

Something wonderful can happen
Any time or any day,
And the things we hope and pray for
May be 'just a night away,'
For no matter what the day holds,
Or how hopeless things may seem,
There can be a 'bright tomorrow'
With new dreams for us to dream.

This might suggest the Bible text: "These are new every morning" or "Thou shalt be secure, for there is hope . . ." to the receiver, or the wonderful old quote: "Never think that God's delays are God's denials."

Now, one that does use a Bible text on the left page inside. The title:

THINKING OF YOU

"A friend loveth at all times"
Life isn't all sunshine,
It isn't all showers,
But they are both needed
To give us the flowers,
And there's always sunshine
That follows the rain
To make the days brighter
And happy again!

The writer, in using this particular Bible text, indicates love and understanding and gives the receiver assurance of a brighter day. Like so many inspirational cards, this one may be used for many occasions — maybe an unfilled hope, maybe an unhappy circumstance, maybe in sympathy.

Examples could go on and on; I've only scratched the surface. We use many inspirational sentiments in anniversary and wedding, birth congratulations, convalescents, cheer cards, and all seasonals. By now, you should have some ideas of your own for inspirational sentiments. My feeling about inspirationals may not be just like Hallmark's, Gibson's, or Rust Craft's, so it's good to research all lines before you try any. They are all similar in feeling, but you may find something in each of our lines that seems to indicate the type each of us might choose — and you might sell. Study the inspirationals a little more carefully even than you do other types of sentiments for they *must* have that *spark* that makes them *inspirational* — and it's something you have to *feel* in your heart!

Chapter VII

Short and Sweet...Informal Cards

by Agnes

Informal cards, also known as *cutes,* are the hardest of all greeting cards to define. They are neither humorous nor inspirationals, conventional nor studio, fish nor fowl. They lie, as Rod Serling might say, somewhere in the twilight zone of greeting cards.

In general, they are not as sentimental as conventional cards, though they may be sweeter; and they are not as punchy or funny as studio cards, but they are more sentimental. On a comparison basis, they might be defined as somewhat sweet and soft-humored studio cards, though they may have a different shape than studio cards.

Basically, you can use the same humor writing techniques on cute, or informal, cards as you can on studio cards. For example, truth, whimsy, exaggeration, play-on-words, reverse, and so on. You simply don't try for the hard, punchy humor. Instead, you try for the soft, sweet, cute, gentle, amusing, nice kind of humor. For example, here are a couple of Barker cards:

> (Two cute characters sipping soda from a
> single glass)
> Just being friends . . .
> . . . is a wonderful part of living!

> (Cute sad-faced character with a tear
> drop under one eye)
> Without you . . .
> . . . I'm the loneliest person in town.

And here are some Gibson cards that that very talented and nice editor, Margaret Gould, feels are representative of good cute ideas. (Notice in these how the basic humor writing formulas show up.)

(Play-on-words)
> (A cute couple in white wigs and early-American
> ballroom clothes dancing)
> Thinking of you . . .
> . . . every MINUET!

(Truth — or maybe Exaggeration)
> (A cute character standing on a globe of the
> world)
> There are more than *Three Billion People* in
> this *World* . . .
> . . . and you're one of the nicest!

One point I'm certain you've already noticed is how tightly the text is tied in to the illustration. This doesn't happen often in studio cards where the text can usually stand alone, or in conventional cards where a dozen different illustrations might go with any one verse. This is basically a *cute* card trademark. So when writing your ideas, think *visually* and try to write your idea so that it can be tied to a cute illustration . . . it will greatly increase your chances of selling.

Now let's look at some more Gibson cards.

(Play-on-words coupled to illustration)
> (A cute toy horse)
> Forget YOUR birthday? . . .
> . . . NEIGH!

(Whimsy)
> (A humorous bulldog holding a rose
> in his mouth)
> I get so SENTIMENTAL . . .
> . . . over birthdays! HOPE YOURS IS ROSY!

(Play-on-words coupled to illustration)
      (Cute little angel sitting among a
      morning glory plant)
      GLORY BE! . . .
      . . . IT'S YOUR BIRTHDAY! Have a Happy!
(Reverse)

      (Toy French poodle)
      Hope your Birthday's just SO-SO . . .
      . . . HAPPY!

The name that a company gives to these types of cards might give you a clue to the kind of ideas to write for them. For example, Barker calls their cute cards *Tender Greetings.* And one of the names Gibson uses is *Happy-Go-Lightly.* So when you're looking at these cards on the racks, check the back of the cards and see if the company has given the cards a special name. It could set the tone of the ideas for you.

Here are some Barker cards:

(Truth)

      (A cute character wearing a huge hat with
      a birthday cake on it)
      It's easy to remember a birthday . . .
      . . . for someone as nice as you.

(Truth)

      (A cute little girl holding flowers
      and wearing them in her hat)
      Just to say "Hi" . . .
      . . . to someone awfully nice to know.

Now that you've read all of these examples, and can see how they all use basic humor formulas, go to Chapter XVI, *How To Get Funny Ideas When You're Alone,* and study the humor writing techniques given there, and then apply them to the soft, cute type of humor used in these cards. The humor writing principles are the same. It's simply a matter of the type of humor used. Work at it, and it will come — as all things do.

Chapter VIII

Be a Kid Again...Juvenile Cards

by Florence F. Bradley

Would you like to be a kid again for a few hours each day, drawing pictures, making things, and playing games — and be well paid for it?

If you have patience, imagination, and understand children, you should try one of the most challenging, creative, and financially rewarding forms of writing today — juvenile greeting cards.

It's a specialized field that involves hard work, research, and time. Sometimes one card takes half a day to do, from the time you think of it, until you figure out all the angles to make it work, test it, and make the card itself.

But the pay runs about $25 to $35 each — and several of mine have made me $50 a piece — and that's not bad, for half a day's work! Besides, they're such fun to do!

Good juvenile writers are hard to find, and if you can come up with original ideas that will hold a child's interest, yet not be too expensive to make, you'll soon find editors asking you to do special assignments — yes, *you!* And this chapter will tell you how to do it.

What *is* a juvenile card? It's a greeting card made especially for a child. There are two basic kinds, verse cards and activity cards.

The first type, verse cards, are just that — a card with a cute illustration on the front, and a verse inside. But it's a special kind of verse that uses colorful words and is musically pleasing to the ear.

If your verse is about a child, give him a name. If you're writing about an animal, give it a funny name — the funnier, the better. For instance, this verse I did for Easter:

> This is Blabbit the Rabbit,
> And he's come to say,
> Someone as nice as you deserves
> A happy Easter day!

Talk to children on their own level. Call a girl a young miss, not a sweet little girl, and a boy a fine young man, not a dear little boy. And be up-to-date with your verse subjects! Except for the very young child, where it used to be downy ducks and teddy bears, today's well-informed youngster goes for rocket ships and astronauts.

You can sometimes help to sell a verse by suggesting it be made into a mechanical card. That is, it would have something moving in some way, when the card is opened.

The three to nine-year-olds especially love mechanicals. If you write a verse about a boy playing football, carry through on your idea, and as the card is opened, have his leg come up and kick the football. A juvenile verse about a cat will sell faster if you have the cat move in some way, when the card is opened.

A verse that ties in with an illustration, will also have a good chance of selling. Like this one that went to Paramount:

> With a ha-ha-ha and a ho-ho-ho,
> Santa's sleigh glides over the snow.
> To bring lots of toys and Christmas cheer
> To a Grandson who is very dear!

Can't you just see Santa in his sleigh, laughing out loud, as he makes his rounds on Christmas Eve?

Most companies prefer cute, colorful verse, preferably not longer than eight lines. Keep your verses general, so the card could be sent to *any* little girl, or *any* little boy. Simplicity in style; this is the keynote for today's verses, like this little two-liner that Buzza-Cardozo bought:

> For Baby on Valentine's Day
>
> Although you're really very small,
> You're the sweetest Valentine of all!

Included in the verse category, is the age series. This is the card that starts out: Today you're one, today you're two, today you're three, etc., and uses the child's age as a basis for the verse itself. Nearly every company has an age series, which they buy verses for.

You'll find, however, that even *these* usually have a stand-up figure or rocking-horse type of set up, or a button with the child's age on it. So the trend in juvenile greeting cards is definitely towards the largest selling type of card: the "idea" or activity card. This is the greeting card that gives a child something to do or play with. It's pretty much what the juvenile greeting card market is all about.

There are several kinds of activity cards: games, quizzes and puzzles, and things to make or do.

A game card that I designed last winter, originated when I saw a field mouse running across the snow. I wondered if a cat would get him before he found a warm place to hide. "That's an idea for a game card," I thought. So I dashed to my desk, and made a list of all the things I could think of that could delay a little mouse trying to get in out of the snow. Here are some that I came up with:

> He could fall into a snowbank
> He could get caught in a mousetrap
> A cat could get him
> He could stop to eat a piece of cheese

Next, I wondered, "How could this be made into a greeting card?" Putting two little mice in the bottom left-hand corner of the card, I made spaces back and forth, across the card (with tiny mouse tracks in them, just for effect) that led to a nice warm house in the top right-hand corner. I played around with this for a while, and decided the game should be played by two children, each trying to get their mouse into the house first, by picking up little cards telling them how many spaces to move. They would try to avoid getting caught by each of the obstacles mentioned above, plus many others I came up with. After *my* children tried the game and gave it their *"Seal of Approval,"* I put a verse on the front:

Birthdays are a fun day,
And so I've sent to you,
A *wish* for a fun day
And a game that's fun to *do*.

Then I sent it to an editor. I hope the little mouse in the field found a warm place to live. He made me $25!

Quizzes and puzzles make good get well cards. A bed-ridden youngster welcomes a challenge, to break the monotony. I got just such an idea from a pet shop that's not too far from our house. One day I wandered inside to see a pair of white huskies from Alaska, or wherever huskies come from. I was impressed with the varieties of dogs they had there. There seemed to be one from nearly every country. Suddenly I had an idea for a quiz card.

At home, I got out my Golden Book Dictionaries (more about them later), looked up dogs, and found half a page of them! Sure enough, they came from all different countries.

When I made the card, I drew all types of dogs all around it, with a list of countries in the middle. The child was to draw

a line from the dog to its nationality. (English bull, Irish set-
ter, etc.) The verse topped off the idea:

> The day goes slow when you're in bed!
> You'd rather be outside, instead.
> So all these dogs have come to play
> And help you pass the time away.

And my card was finished. A most profitable trip to the pet
store!

Notice that the verse on the front of an activity card tends
to tie in with the activity inside, giving the child some idea of
what is coming.

The next type of activity card, has something to make or do.
Here's how one of mine came about:

My daughter had been given a shot for virus, and she got even
with the doctor by drawing a very unflattering picture of him, with
a long hypodermic needle in his hand. I turned the idea over
in my mind while I did the dishes. Most children like to draw,
and they certainly have time to when they're sick in bed.

I made my daughter a *dummy* card, just to try out my idea.
On the front, I printed:

> You're sick?
> Well just don't lay there feeling sad!
> Being sick isn't all that bad!
> So get a pencil and begin
> And I'll bet your pictures bring a grin!

Inside, I wrote:

> This is my doctor (He's making me well)

And I left a space for her to draw her doctor. Next, it said:

> This is my mommy (She's treating me swell!)
> This is my medicine (It don't taste the best)
> And this one is me (Getting lots of rest.)

My daughter was delighted, and asked me to make another

one. I did — but this time I sent it off to an editor. And she bought it.

I guess the most important thing in writing juvenile activity cards is getting good ideas. Where do I get ideas for my cards? Just about everywhere. Children's books and magazines are a good place to start. You can often find an idea in a book or magazine, change it around, and come up with something new and appealing.

Television and movies are another good source of ideas. Children's games can often be adapted to greeting cards. Many of my children's cards come from games I played in my childhood, sometimes putting a new twist on an old idea.

Perhaps most of all, I *really* pay attention to the everyday situations around me, and adapt them for juvenile cards.

Let's take a look at some of the successful ideas I've derived from the above sources, and sold to various greeting card companies.

First on the list is children's books and magazines. I have a set of Golden Book Dictionaries that are worth their weight in gold. Their illustrations are wonderful. If I'm not sure how many toes to put on the animal I'm drawing, or which way the stripes go on a zebra, I can always find out by looking it up in my dictionaries. When I'm stuck for ideas, leafing through a volume or two usually gives me several.

Childrens' magazines are an excellent place to look for salable ideas. Humpty Dumpty has many mechanical things to do, and I've gotten many ideas from it. Jack and Jill once gave me an idea that resulted in a $75 sale for three cards, all based on the same idea. Here's how it happened.

My children's copy of Jack and Jill was lying on the floor and when I picked it up, I noticed a little Halloween story that had blanks in it, every other sentence or so. I remembered playing that as a child, and my money brain decided to try it for a greeting card. At the time Barker Greeting Cards was doing Valentines, so I wrote the following little Valentine story:

> Cupid had a problem. His two favorite friends, John, who just loves ...., and Joan, who is very much like ...., didn't have Valentines to love! Every one needs .... to be happy on Valentine's Day! Cupid set out to solve the problem. He sent .... the color of .... to Joan, and he signed it from .... Then he shot .... from his bow at John. Next, Cupid mixed a love potion of .... and .... And he stirred it with .... Then he put some in .... for Joan, and the rest into .... for John. And it worked! Before you could say ...., Joan and John fell in love. They got married on St. Valentine's Day, and they sent Cupid .... to say "Thank you."

I had little words and phrases such as a pet frog, a spoon, a cupcake, a flower, a car, a tree, a bathtub, the front porch, sugar, money, the Jolly Green Giant, a cardboard box, a secret, and a blue bottle, which were to be cut out and inserted in the blanks as the story was read. Changing the sequence of the words and phrases makes the story come out differently every time you read it. Try it.

The editor at Barker (who, incidentally, is the editor of this book) liked it well enough to ask me to make two more cards like it — one with a Christmas story, and one with an Easter story.

Let's take a look at getting ideas from movies and television. When James Bond and 007 became popular, I wanted to tie in an idea for the older boys (from 9-12) with the famous detective. I know this age group is interested in challenging things like sports or mysteries to solve, and finally hit on a decoding wheel that could be used to decode a Valentine message inside the card, and also to send secret messages to friends. The verse on the front, tied it in with the hero of the day.

> We're both secret agents
> And the message I've sent,
> Is in secret code, so —
> To find what I meant,
> You'll have to de-code it,
> — Look inside for the way.
> And see what I'm wishing
> For Valentine's Day!

By the time this one sold, I'd had to make the decoding wheel for my sons and half of their friends. It was very big in our neighborhood.

The Philadelphia 76'ers basketball team has a lot of fans at our house, and for a while there, it seemed like every time I turned around, there was another basketball game on television. Finally I gave in, and watched one. Gee, it looked like fun, throwing that ball through the hoops!

Always looking for greeting card ideas, I tried to figure out how to put the game on a card, and devised a cardboard set-up that had two basketball hoops inside, to be cut out and bent to stand up. It had circles to be cut out to pitch pennies or buttons through.

My only problem, was that the game took up the entire inside of the card, leaving no room for instructions. So I had to be sure that the verse on the front explained what the card was about. I came up with this one that filled the bill:

> You're getting to be such a big boy and all,
> I've sent this game of basketball.
> With a little cutting, a few small bends,
> And you're ready to play it with your friends.

Now I'm a 76'ers fan, too!

Next we come to *games* that can be adapted for greeting

cards. The first game that pops into my tired brain is *bingo*. I sold that one not only once, but twice! — thanks to my four-year-old. She wanted to play bingo with the older children, and they told her, "You can't play, you don't know your numbers."

Trying to comfort her, I said, "I'll make you a bingo game you can play!" And I did. The game had colors on the cards instead of numbers. A spinner was provided, and each time a child spun a color, he was allowed to cover one square of that color on his card. It worked very well and, with the following verse, brought me a tidy sum as a juvenile greeting card:

> I hope you have fun on your birthday,
> And to help make sure you do,
> I picked this special birthday card
> With a game inside for you.

Looking through my "sold" file a few months later, (another place to get ideas) I came across the color bingo game. I was doing juvenile Christmas cards, and I decided to try the bingo idea again, this time using pictures of toys instead of numbers. It was fun, tied in with the season, and could be played by all children — for what child doesn't know toys?

The verse on that one read:

> HI THERE! MERRY CHRISTMAS!
> No need to wait till Christmas,
> Start having fun right now.
> Play Santa's brand-new Bingo game,
> Inside tells you how . . .

This was one of the cards that took nearly half a day to do, drawing all those little toys on the bingo cards. When I started doing juvenile greeting cards — several years ago — I couldn't draw worth a darn. But I soon found that the cards I took the time to illustrate brought me the most money, so I kept trying, and it gets easier as I go along. If you can't draw very well either, don't be discouraged — keep doing the best you can; you can get by with just enough of an illustration to help put your idea across to the editor. And you'll find it becomes easier with practice. Besides, those fatter checks make it well worth the time!

A good way to get started doing juvenile cards is to delve into your own childhood. You've probably seen paper dolls and punch-out cowboys on children's cards. They're very good sellers. Why? Because adults buy the cards that are sent to children, and most adults played paper dolls or cowboys when they were children. They remember nostalgically the old and familiar games they played, so they buy the cards that have them. Appeal to the adult, and your card will be a good seller. For that reason, many of my children's cards were based on things I enjoyed as a child, and that my children enjoy doing now.

For instance, one evening while sitting on my front steps watching my daughters play hopscotch, I got the bright idea that that too could be turned into a juvenile activity card. The problem was to get hopscotch, which took up my whole sidewalk, onto a little card about ten or eleven inches wide. I used the regular hopscotch pattern in miniature and had my children try to toss pennies into each square, without landing on the lines. The first one to get all the way to the end, won the game. They liked it.

I called it Penny Hopscotch, added a verse:

> Get a penny for you
> and one for a pal,
> And play penny hopscotch,
> inside tells you how!

— and promptly turned the idea into a check from Gibson Greetings. (Incidentally, I did the same thing with shuffleboard, using pencils and buttons and a miniature shuffleboard.)

So, what games did *you* enjoy as a child? Maybe they're worth money in the juvenile activity card market!

Juvenile cards are done in about three age groups — the 3-6, 6-9, and 9-12 age levels. So when I'm working on juveniles, I try to do some the older child will enjoy, and some for the younger child. For instance, this quiz I did with the younger children in mind, popped into my head when one of my children printed her name. The letters were all there, but in the wrong order. I had been looking for ideas for Christmas activity cards and used the idea of scrambled names. The verse explains the card:

A CHRISTMAS PROBLEM

Santa went shopping and bought four pair
Of pretty collars for his reindeer to wear.
He painted them quick, before the reindeer could see
But he got the names scrambled as they can be.

Of course, inside were the collars waiting for the child to unscramble the names on them. As usual, I put the correct answers inside the card, in case the child got stuck.

As I said before, one of the best ways I've been successful getting ideas for juvenile greeting cards, is by observing what goes on around me every day and adapting these things to cards. (Of course it helps to have six children to get ideas from!)

Let me show you what I mean: One day I was watching my teenage daughter and the girl next door, trying out different hairstyles to see which one they liked best. At first I thought they were just amusing, then the more I thought of it — what teenage girl doesn't like to try out different hairdos? I decided to try the idea on a teenager's birthday card.

How, I wondered, could I have a girl on a card changing her hairstyle, in a way that the girl receiving the card could participate in the changes, rather than just turning the pages and seeing different hairdos?

I played around with this idea for quite a while before I came up with a special-fold card that had a girl's face on the middle page, and as each page folded over it, it was cut out so that the girl's face showed through. As each page folded over, it gave her a different hairdo. One was a paper hairdo that was curled around a pencil, and came out in a flip. Another page had red wool, and was to be braided into pigtails. One was yellow felt, and could be trimmed shorter, etc. The verse brought out the fact that the problem of the right hairdo, is universal:

> HAPPY BIRTHDAY TO A KEEN TEEN
> I know sometimes you can't decide
> Which hair style's best for you.
> If you help solve Kathy's problem,
> Perhaps you'll solve yours, too!

Another idea that brought me a tidy sum, came to me when we were out fishing one day. One of the younger children couldn't seem to catch anything, and decided that it was just too hard for him to do.

When we got home, I came up with little cardboard fish with holes in their noses to catch them with. Their tails were inserted in a cardboard pond with slits in it, and a fishing pole made of a string and a safety pin, completed my fishing game for my little guy. He enjoyed catching fish this way so well, I sent it to Rust Craft, and *it* wound up as a greeting card, too:

> It's lots of fun to go fishing
> And if that is your wish,
> Then you are really lucky —
> With your *own* pond of fish!

I think one of the best ideas I ever came up with, was one that saved me a lot of back-breaking work. We were making a snowman in our front yard, and as he got bigger and bigger, Mommy was the first one to get tired. As I staggered into the house for a cup of hot chocolate, I thought, "There must be an easier way to make a snowman!"

Leave it to tired old me to come up with one, and naturally, once I did, it found its way onto a greeting card! It turned out to be a game that the whole family could enjoy. On the front of the card all I had to put was a big picture of a snowman, complete with a top hat, and the words:

> Mr. Snowman and I bring you Christmas fun.

Inside, was a spinner, with a head, buttons, top hat — the works — on it. The object: To be first to spin a complete snowman like the one on the front of the card.

Now when the kids say, "Mom, let's make a snowman," I dig out the greeting card snowman game, and that's that, as far as I'm concerned!

There is a special way to come up with ideas for seasonal cards for the juvenile greeting card market. I make a list of all the things that have to be done, say — for Christmas — and a list of all the things I can think of in connection with the season, such as holly, tree, candles, etc. And I re-read these lists until something jells in my mind and gives me an idea for a card. For instance, I got $50 for an original Christmas game that I came up with using this method:

> The card had two Christmas trees inside, and a spinner. On the spinner was tinsel, balls, an angel, candy canes, etc. Several of each of these things were pictured on little markers to be cut out, also. Whenever a child spun something he needed to trim his tree, he took a marker with that item on it, and placed it on his tree. First one to trim his tree, won. Original? Yes. Fun for a child? Yes. Time-consuming to make? Yes. But profitable for me! . . . and, I hope, for the greeting card company, too!

This same company took an original game I did that had children drawing cards to complete their Christmas shopping lists. Both of these ideas came from my "list of things to do." Everyone has a gift list to complete. Just about everyone trims a tree for Christmas. Making a list of these things could easily give you an idea for still another type of Christmas game. Try it! (You might also get the idea for a "trimming the Christmas tree game," while you're trimming your tree in December, but when July rolls around and you're doing Christmas cards, you forget that stuff. Hence the lists.)

An important thing to remember about original game cards is that you are the only one who knows how the game is to be played. Write down the rules. Study them. Then re-write them, giving clear, simple directions that a child can understand. Make sure everything the child needs to know to play the game is there.

Then give the game to a child or two, preferably about the age the card is intended for. Let them read the directions and play the game. Alone.

You may be surprised. Your rules may be far from clear. Or you may need more markers or little cards than you thought. Some ideas simply will not work out. And some games just are not fun after all. Now is your chance to fix them up, or scrap them, *before* an editor sees them.

As an example, let's look at the directions I gave for the Christmas tree game I just mentioned:

> Trim the Christmas Tree. (For two players.)
> You each take turns spinning to get the
> decorations you need to trim your Christmas
> tree. The first player who trims his
> tree wins. To win, you must get:
> 4 balls (1 each of green, yellow, red, and blue.)
> 2 tinsels
> 2 candy canes
> 1 angel for tree top

Each time you spin, put the decoration the spinner
points to on your tree. (There are extra decorations
in case you lose some.) If you spin a blank or a
decoration you already have, you lose that turn and
the other player spins.

Let me inject a bit of my own philosophy here. There are two
rules you should always remember about doing games for juvenile
greeting cards. Always make sure your work is original, and
always, *always* test it before you send it out. I have talked to
nearly every editor I've ever sold to. They *try* the games. They
do the quizzes and puzzles. You'd be surprised how many of
my games wouldn't have sold if I hadn't found out before hand
that they weren't quite workable at first. If you don't have
children around, play the game yourself. Take the place of each
player. A good idea is to put blanks in for lost turns to make
a game last longer, and for more suspense. Put the answers to
quizzes and puzzles inside the cards, — the editor shouldn't
have to figure it out — and make sure you didn't forget anything.

It's hard work. You can't afford to spend half a day on an
idea that isn't good. Carbon copies of other cards on the market
won't sell.

Besides, there is no end of places to get ideas. Look at the
world as a child does. There are dozens of ideas on the toy
counters of the 5 & 10, waiting to be adapted to juvenile cards.
Watch the children around you. I sold a "penny saver" card
when I saw my son working on his coin collection. I did a puzzle
in the shape of a heart for Valentines Day. I sold a card for
children in bed to make shadow pictures on the wall. And watching children look for the golden egg in an Easter egg hunt
resulted in a game card that sold to Hallmark.

If you have a good, original game, puzzle, or quiz but are
afraid the verse on it isn't good enough, send it in any way. A
good verse won't sell a poor idea, but if your activity is good

and your verse doesn't measure up, you may get a check for the idea, but find the company has returned your verse, preferring to do its own.

Occasionally, a company (Rust Craft is one) will buy a story up to about 300 words for use on a story-book greeting card. But usually, old stand-bys like "Peter Rabbit" are used.

After your cards have made the rounds, try to improve on the ones that haven't sold, and send them out again, a year later. If they still don't sell and you think they have merit, cut off the verses, and send just the game or idea part to children's magazines or Sunday School papers that buy fillers. They may not bring as much as cards, but they'll help pay back the postage money!

If, as happens, you have a game that is really good, but too expensive for a company to put on a greeting card, send it to a game manufacturer. Maybe you'll sell it there.

You can see there are lots of ways to make money in the juvenile activity card or verse market. It's well worth the effort, for the pay is very good. Besides, it's certainly a great feeling when you get one of *your* finished cards in the mail from a thoughtful editor. Or find one unexpectedly on a counter in your own neighborhood. And the first time you send one of *your* cards to your own favorite youngster, you won't trade this business for any other in the world.

Chapter IX

Writing Humorous Cards

by Ray Mathews

Since you're interested in writing humorous cards I guess I can safely assume that you have a sense of humor . . . and a sense of humor can be a tremendous asset as you laugh yourself through the trials and errors of learning your craft. Writing humorous cards for money isn't quite as funsy-wunsy as all that. Oh sure, it's a great business and I've enjoyed every minute of it. But it is work. Hard work.

Just what *is* a humorous card? A humorous card is one that expresses a sentiment in a funny, clever, or cute way. It can be hilarious, slap-stick, witty, comical, or just lighthearted. Don't worry too much about specific definitions from the start. With enough observation, practice, and experience you'll learn to recognize a humorous card when you see one. Humorous cards are quite frequently written around various folds, pop-outs, attachments, flocking, die cuts and other gimmicks almost too numerous to mention. Here, for example, is a humorous card I sold to Gibson:

TO MY HUBBY

Sometimes we go on WARPATH
But then when we're all done . . .
Making up in WIGWAM
IS HEAP BIG HAPPY FUN!

The outside of the card illustrates a Chief and Squaw having an argument. The inside shows the same couple kissing and making up in a wigwam. The fact that the wigwam on the inside actually pops out, creating a 3-dimensional effect, contributes handsomely to the card. Now consider all the elements. A woman buys this card for her husband. All normal husbands and wives have arguments. They also delight in making up. Thus, we are working with a realistic, true-to-life situation, a situation with which wives can identify. The Indian characters add humor and color to the illustration. The message is expressed in a simple, four-line verse. The wigwam is a natural for a pop-out. Put 'em all together and you have an attractive 50¢ card.

Now, by contrast, consider this card I sold to Barker:

TO MOM
who has always done so much
to develop personality and character
. . . from the character you helped develop!
HAPPY MOTHER'S DAY!

This sentiment is written in two lines of prose — not verse — and makes use of a little play on the words *develop* and *character*. The first line, on the cover, expresses a sincere and genuine compliment to Mom. Then, on the inside, the sender laughs at himself a bit by referring to himself as a *character*. This is a sentiment with which senders — of both sexes — can easily identify. The only illustration is on the cover and it depicts a cute lady, obviously Mom. It is a simple fold card, very much on the order of the familiar studio card.

It may be worth mentioning at this point that there is frequently an overlapping between humorous and studio ideas — and which type of card your idea will be used on is usually decided by the editor. Perhaps one of the best ways to distinguish between the two areas when they overlap is in the illustration. The humorous illustration will usually be a bit more on the cute side; the studio illustration will be a bit more on the contemporary or stylized side. The humorous card will be somewhat more flexible in size, while the studio card usually conforms to the long rectangular shape.

Here's still another example of a card purchased by Gibson:

SISTERS ARE LIKE RECORDS . . .

Some are cool
And some are square —
Some are great
And some are fair —
Some are weird
And some are sweet —
Some are wild
And some are beat
Some are "in"
But very few are
STRICTLY TOPS
The way that *you* are!
Happy Birthday, Sister!

This idea is expressed in twelve lines of verse and lends itself naturally to illustration. Comparing sisters to records is highly appealing, especially to the younger customers who are very record conscious. Each descriptive word — cool, square, etc. — is applicable to both sisters and records. Finally, in the last two lines, the *punch* of the verse is achieved. The sender compliments the sister by telling her that she's TOPS! This is an example of a card where a multiple fold was utilized so that the idea was illustrated over an area of five pages — colorful and appealing.

Perhaps by now you have developed some idea of how humorous greeting cards are written and what elements actually go into their creation. The first example was expressed in four lines of verse; the second was expressed in two lines of prose; the third was expressed in twelve lines of verse — three very different approaches to the development of humorous card ideas.

The great thing about writing humorous greeting cards is that you have so much flexibility. There are almost no limitations to the creation of ideas. The important thing to keep in mind, however, is that you adhere to the time-tested principle that all greeting cards should contain a *me-to-you* message. Be sincere, be natural, and always keep the *identity* factor in mind — the sender should identify with the receiver, and the receiver should identify with the sentiment or gag. Get these double identifications into your cards and you'll sell a lot more of them.

Take a Barker card for example:

> MOM —
> I like my eggs sunny side up . . .
> My cereal with sliced bananas . . .
> My hamburgers with relish . . .
> My ice cream with chocolate syrup . . .
> . . . BUT I LIKE YOU JUST THE WAY YOU ARE!
> HAPPY MOTHER'S DAY!

Here the sender identifies herself again with Mom, the great provider of food and other assorted goodies, but in the last line she switches from her stomach to her heart by saying "I like you just the way you are," a most sincere compliment. The entire message is expressed in prose. It's sincere, it's natural and thousands upon thousands of people — sons, daughters and mothers — can easily identify themselves with this sentiment. An extra plus is the fact that a little frying pan containing two eggs is attached to the cover and appears to be in the hands of a cute lady, obviously representing Mom. The opening line of copy "I like my eggs sunny side up" ties in beautifully with this attachment.

How does all this help *you* write humorous greeting cards? Well, first of all, I would suggest that you take time to review the four examples of card ideas I've presented and explained up to this point. Take the first example. Are there any other ways you can express this same basic sentiment? Consider again the relationship between a husband and a wife. They sometimes disagree. They argue. Yes, they battle! But how they love to make up! Could you think of some characters *other* than Indians to represent the husband and wife for the sake of illustration and color? Hillbillies, maybe? How about considering the use of an attachment instead of a pop-out? Would you prefer to express your sentiment in prose rather than verse? What about *other* basic elements of a husband-wife relationship? What do they like to do? Where do they like to go? What is universally familiar to most husbands and wives? Think these things out. Get them down on paper. Work them over.

Now do the same with the other examples. Review them. Study the various comments pertinent to them. How can these ideas be improved upon? Think of the people in your own life — relatives, friends. What would you say to them on some special occasion such as a birthday or an anniversary? Always try to be as funny as possible, but never sacrifice the sentiment for the sake of humor itself. Being funny merely for the sake of being funny is meaningless in greeting card writing. Too many writers at the start tend to make the mistake of concentrating too much on the humor and too little on the sentiment. Once you train yourself to think automatically in terms of a me-to-you message, the humor elements will begin to fall into place. But like all crafts and professions, writing greeting card humor requires a considerable amount of practice.

Here's a Gibson example for you to consider:

ON YOUR BIRTHDAY

Don't be a goody-goody —
Don't be a silly prude —
'Cause there's no time like your birthday . . .
To get in a PARTY MOOD!
HAPPY BIRTHDAY!

The cover illustration depicts a cute dog with a golden halo over his head. The look on his face is one of sweet innocence. The inside illustrates the same dog holding a cocktail glass, whooping it up. He's wearing the proverbial lamp shade on his head and as the card is opened, the lamp shade pops up over the top of the card creating a delightfully novel effect. This is just another way of the sender telling the receiver: It's your birthday so let your hair down and have a blast — or have fun — enjoy yourself — live it up.

When writing your humorous card ideas, use all of the humor formulas given in Chapter XVI: exaggeration, play-on-words, whimsy, and all the others. Even though most of your ideas will be in verse, the humor formulas remain the same, both in principle and application.

Verse for humorous cards should have all the feel of good *light verse*. It should not be heavy and ponderous, it should be light and playful, with rhymes and meters that have a bounce to them. Two excellent books for humorous card writers are: for rhyming words and techniques of versification, Clement Wood's *The Complete Rhyming Dictionary;* and, for techniques of writing light verse, Richard Armour's *Writing Light Verse*.

Study the examples in this chapter, and the humor formulas in Chapter XVI over and over again. Then go out and browse around a card shop and examine the numerous approaches successful writers are using in the creation and development of humorous cards. Keep your eyes opened for ideas in magazines, newspapers, books, and on TV — to mention just a few sources where you might discover a fresh thought for a greeting card. Write something every day — good, bad, or indifferent — but *write*. Your good ideas will begin to take shape as you apply yourself to your craft.

Have fun!

Chapter X

How to Write Studio Cards
and Still Have Time Left for Sex

by Bob Hammerquist

You'd like to write studio cards? Well, bless your little starry eyes . . .

As a card-carrying free lancer, I will now force feed you with a few of my conclusions about studios, editors, and the System as seen from the wrong side of the New York-New Haven-and-Hartford Railroad. Having, for the occasion, through an extraordinary application of will power on my part, raised the blood content of my Scotch to a preposterous level, I would appreciate your not zonking out for at least a few paragraphs. What I put before you are my own opinions, it is only fair to say, and are not to be confused, necessarily, with reality. However, I have faked my way through this thing for a good ten years now, narrowly missing the Alms House in the process, and this alone, it seems to me, demands a minimal respect on the part of apprentice charlatans.

Compared to the more traditional types of greeting cards, the studio format is still quite new, a mere teenager, but it has been around long enough now to be accepted by most card buyers, dealers, and manufacturers as a reasonably honest American product (which, in case you have never actually seen one in print before, is an authentic left-handed compliment). The exact birth date of studios is pretty hazy. They just seemed to "appear" in the early fifties, coming from any number of small, independent and somewhat adventuresome types who wanted a new way to say Greeting Cards. The huge and near-huge manufacturers at first looked upon the studios as something akin to a New Leftist at the 35th Class Reunion, but their collective health was good and it seems they may live to a ripe and irreverent old age after all. However, with a prognosis of longevity, and with their present image as a profit maker, 2,850,000 card manufacturers have, as of this date, laid claim to their birth. Nothing breeds like success, as they chant at the big league fertility rites. There are, naturally, a few holdouts in and out of the business who still consider the studios a mere house of cards waiting for a zephyr. Yet, studios are here and hearty.

Can you write them? Well, if you're the cool, unflappable, methodical, efficient, reasoning type, I submit that this is not your pasture. You could probably make a go of it, but it would be work. And it shouldn't be work. It is almost essential that you have a few parts missing . . . or, at least, not working properly.

Now, before you jog off in a tri-colored snit, please don't dismiss all the advice given you as irrelevant. Throughout this book and even in this chapter — verily and gasp — there will be a few little dainties it would be good to pay attention to because you just can't get around them. I just don't want you to approach this writing experience (if you'll excuse the expression) wrapped in layers of cumbersome regulations that only work in theory. Read the books, but don't memorize them.

First of all, let's take a look at your sense of humor. Like, have you got one? Of course you do, you say, or you wouldn't be reading this to see how it can be applied. Well, look coldly at it again. Remember, at the cocktail party everyone thinks he or she personally is a riot, or even better, a wry wit. Most teetotalers also suffer from this delusion, you may have noticed.

Oiled or dry, most of them just lie there. So, to the extent that it is possible to evaluate objectively your own sense of humor, give it a good try. Most people do have some type of funny bone, true. Everyone thinks *something* is funny. Different things for different people, naturally, but I would venture that most of us have, shall we say, a limited humor quotient. Some, to be sure, more limited than others.

What about you? Can you laugh at, or at least "appreciate" the different types of humor presented in various situations? Do you dig the more sophisticated (yes, I know, thank you, that *is* a relative word) comedians and satirical reviews that zap away at societal shortcomings? And because this is your cup of tea, do you find the Red Skelton-Jackie Gleason-Bob Hope syndrome inane and beneath your standards? Or is it the other way around? Do you like — and I mean really *like* — sight gags, burlesque, humor, an inflated pig's bladder ricocheting off someone's ear? What about S. J. Perelman or Jean Shepherd — funny writers? How about Political humor? Religious humor? Ethnic humor? Blue humor? Yes? No? Nice, neat divisions, everything marked GOOD or BAD?

Well, if you plan to write studio cards, and make a few clams at it, it doesn't hurt to appreciate as many styles and types of humor as possible. There are outlets for all of them. Risque ideas or slightly blue material can be outrageously funny or plain smut masquerading as humor. Satire and parody can be subtle and penetratingly funny. They can also be smug, bitter, self-righteous, and just plain dull. If you can understand and like good humor at any level, your job as an idea writer will be that much easier.

Don't Get Discouraged — Part I. No one writer is all things to all editors. Everyone has a flair for writing certain types of material better than others. Women, for the most part, turn out delicate, whimsical little gems that makes me want to cry . . . because I can't do them . . . except by accident. You know the kind I mean, the delicate as opposed to the boffo, the cute, soft little ideas that most men have a tough time appreciating, let alone writing. What chance do some of us have against that? Occasionally, we all stumble into an area where we shouldn't be and come up with a nugget, but it's a rarity — to be recognized and capitalized on, nevertheless!

Here are a few examples of the softer type idea that I've clubbed into life.

> COVER: (Neuter character with big smile)
> You're all charm
> INSIDE: . . . and a smile wide!!!
> HAPPY BIRTHDAY

> COVER: I like you . . . you're so . . . so . . . so . . .
> INSIDE: . . . 'phisticated

> COVER: (Cute neuter)
> Psssst . . . Hey you . . .
> INSIDE: . . . you is sexy!

By instinct, however, I am personally from the Bedroom — Belly Button — Bedpan School, and before you look down your freckled beak at that, let me tell you it is rather fun. Simply put, I am betting that bathrooms and bedrooms will be around approximately as long as navels and, unless you are a 32nd degree prig, you might agree that onrushing generations are going to discover, much to their delight, what our peers already know, namely that some very funny things, indeed, do happen in these areas. Not that much really happens in a navel, but what, after all, is a sillier part of the human anatomy? (Well! That's *your* opinion, baby . . .!) And the more you look into it the sillier it gets. (As my Great Uncle Sigurd once observed . . . a navel doesn't happen, a navel *is*!!! As a matter of fact, he squeaked that one out just seconds before they packed him in ice and shipped him off beyond Chicago somewhere. He seemed happy enough. It worked out good for all of us.)

Feast on a few bedroom, belly button, bathroom ideas . . .

COVER: (Man & woman)
It's your ANNIVERSARY . . . *Don't just stand there!*
INSIDE: *CONNUBULATE!!!*
Congratulations!

COVER: (Nude neuter lying on back with candle in navel)
HAPPY BIRTHDAY
INSIDE: . . . silly!

COVER: (Neuter)
Gee, I'm really sorry to hear you're sick . . . is there anything I can do?
INSIDE: . . . like sweep out your bedpan or something?
GET WELL SOON!

(A word of warning! Please, please, please don't flood the market with belly button gags, bedpan gags or sex gags!!! There is no *outstanding* shortage in these particular categories. In fact, most editors would probably cringe at the thought of tons of them coming their way all of a sudden, simply because most ideas in these categories are so definitely awful. But if you've got a *good* one . . .)

Now, please don't sit right down in a creative heat wave and start writing. Heah come de advice! Get out where the cards are! Get out to the card racks in the stores and see what's being done! Don't just browse through a few studios you've saved from a couple of years back. Go out and look at the fresh ones until those starry eyes of yours, as well as your arches, go numb. Not just to your favorite or nearby shops, or the ones closest to the liquor store, but to as wide a variety of outlets as you can find . . . book shops, gift shops, college shops, variety stores, top quality department stores, discount houses, joke shops, tobacco shops . . . anywhere! You'll find quite a variety in the types of studio cards being sold, from the more reserved (Mmmmm!) to the more earthy (Ah Haa!!!) This may sound terribly obvious, but the thing is — are you going to follow up on it? Get out there! Keep getting out there! There's nothing like it to get some idea of what studios are all about.

Now that we're in the store, what are we looking for? No hard core specifics here, but a couple of generalities to keep in the back of your mind. Least important — but imporant enough — are the cards *funny?* Remember now, extend your definition of what might conceivably be funny. After all, you're not supposed to cry or be bored stiff . . . you're supposed to laugh.

Here are a few ideas where, hopefully, the emphasis was on *funny:*

> COVER: (Woman)
> 　　　　So it's your birthday, and you think you're getting
> 　　　　along in years, do you . . . well bless your little heart!
> INSIDE: Sweetie, I've got *girdles* that are older than you!!!
> 　　　　HAPPY DAY!

> COVER: (Just lettering . . . large and bright)
> 　　　　BAAOOM!
> INSIDE: Hark! I think you just went through the FOSSIL BARRIER . . .
> 　　　　HAPPY BIRTHDAY!

> COVER: Having *another* birthday?!
> 　　　　C'mon now, this is getting ridiculous
> INSIDE: 3 more and you're disqualified!
> 　　　　(you know that, don't you)

Secondly, are they short? Most of the good ones are funny (or cute) and as *short* as possible. Very few words, but hopefully, the right words . . . the ones that move the idea across quickly and smoothly without clouding it up. For the most part, these words just don't happen. They have been selected, judged, trimmed, positioned, invented, etc.

For instance . . .

> COVER: I like you . . . you've got *smarts!*
> INSIDE: Your *sexies* aren't bad, either . . .

> COVER: We're related
> INSIDE: . . . and I'm elated!

> COVER: If you don't like this birthday card,
> you can exchange it
> INSIDE: . . . for a bloody nose
> Happy Birthday!

> COVER: By the time you learn to make the most of it . . .
> INSIDE: . . . it's gone!
> HAPPY BIRTHDAY!

Occasionally, however, you will come up with an idea that seems to be funny enough by itself but in order to make it work as a greeting card, you may have to fabricate a fairly lengthy situation . . .

Thusly . . .

> COVER: (Picture of farmer) Farmer Ida
> (Picture of cow) Farmer Ida's cow
> As Farmer Cecil Ida said to his dedicated-
> but-tired-and-feeble old cow, Bessie Mae,
> on the occasion of her twenty-eighth birthday
> INSIDE: . . . HAPPY BIRTHDAY AND NO BULL

> COVER: If you want to live to a ripe old age, follow the
> advice of Zelda Ferbush of North Platte, Nebraska, who
> has eaten an apple a day for all of her 99 years, and
> has this to say about her remarkable practice . . .
> INSIDE: . . . "My sakes . . . if it wasn't for the *booze,* all those
> damn apples would've killed me . . ."
> HAPPY BIRTHDAY

Length is justified in these cases as a mood, a situation, or a plausibility is being constructed for the punch line, but if it doesn't have to be long, don't make it so. Funny and short, if possible!

The essential ingredient we're looking for, though, is *SEND-ABILITY!* Four-star important! The *reason for* a greeting card! It has to be sendable . . . it has to relate to a situation! Somebody's having a birthday, remember? Or someone is sick, or is having an anniversary, or is going on a trip, or is a very special type of friend, or is having a toenail transplant. Something pretty specific. The card buyer is in the shop because of one of these or similar reasons, not to see how clever you are at writing zany abstractions — assuming your abstractions would get by the editors, which they would not. Obviously, card buyers want to communicate with people they care for, and they have chosen studio cards because they want to do so in an informal manner. As a writer, you're simply offering them a choice of messages for the communication. Think about this *constantly* when you're writing card material, for any and all occasions . . . birthdays . . . Christmas, etc. You're *not* writing for a TV or nightclub comedian, or a comic strip, or for any other medium where anything goes. You're writing studio *greeting cards period!* As you write, you might occasionally ask yourself if some unknown person would actually pay out a quarter or fifty cents for this particular idea. Would anyone *steal* it already! Your idea is not standing by itself in the racks, there are hundreds of others lurking about . . . competing! Your idea has to have a number of things in its favor and the most important one is its sendability! Can't get around that.

Here are a few examples of what I would consider sendable greeting cards.

> COVER: If you're pure and chaste, you can be
> my Valentine!
> INSIDE: If you're not, we can certainly work
> out something . . .

COVER: Sorry you're so sick!
INSIDE: Hate to see someone so yummy
feeling so crummy!

COVER: You're like a vintage wine . . . you get
nicer with age . . .
INSIDE: but your keg is starting to swell . . .
HAPPY BIRTHDAY

How do you get ideas? Where do they come from? What's the secret? Occasionally, someone will ask me this, believe it or not. I wish there was a secret, but there isn't. No magic techniques. No polyethylene prayer wheel that spins out the lucky combinations — you'd have contrived ideas, remember? If you feel a need for maxims and do-all devices, maybe you should get into Insurance or Banking or something while there are still a few hours left.

Part of the idea-gathering process is simply keeping your eyes and ears open, and thinking greeting cards twenty-four hours a day. This isn't to say that you run about like a nut obsessed, salivating and pulsating, notebook and pencil in hand. They'd put you in a net. *I'd* put you in a net! No, you go about the business of being an average, urbane, suave, American All-Star, in complete but reserved command of all situations. A beautiful person! A sweetheart! But on some secondary level of awareness, you stay constantly awake to all audible and visual funny business. This may sound like a drag but, after all, it is a job, and a fun one compared to many. It's not Sunday afternoon therapy, girls! Look and listen for the ideas! Simple? Do it, then! TV, radio, movies, theatre, chatter over cocktails and coffee breaks, popular phrases, customs, issues, attitudes and anxieties that reach crests of concern (morality, narcotics, living costs, etc.), articles and cartoons in magazines and newspapers, and office jokes. These are my humble sources resulting in ideas such as these:

> COVER: Happy Birthday to one of the *NOW* PEOPLE!
> INSIDE: From one of the *THEN* PEOPLE!

(At the time of the writing, "Now People" was a popular description of someone young, hip, swinging, etc.)

> COVER: Here's a nice birthday card for you,
>   just to show how tolerant I am!
> INSIDE: Why, some of my best friends are old!!!

(Just another take-off on that old bigot's bromide.)

> COVER: CONGRATULATIONS on your GRADUATION!
> INSIDE: This is the biggest thing since the world's
>   first BELLY BUTTON TRANSPLANT!!!

(Organ transplants have been with us for some time now, to the point where we became quite complacent about them, but the first heart transplants brought everyone to renewed attention. I was forced to reach into my belly button bag once again . . .)

Other greeting cards are also good as idea generators. Not to find ideas that you think you can pilfer (although "creative camouflage" is a legitimate part of this business), but as a general stimulant to put you in a frame of mind. Try it, it'll work.

For instance, browsing through the word play on other cards prompted me to think of some words that could be broken down into two separate and unrelated words that would be so flexible in their combined meaning that almost anything *could be read into them* . . .

> COVER: Happy Valentine's Day
> INSIDE: . . . to someone who makes my TIDDLY WINK!!!

If you have that sense of humor we've talked about, you can't help but see and hear those ideas popping up all around you. People are strange, in case it hasn't come home to you yet. They say and do wild things by design and accident. They are often beautifully unaware of being funny (aren't we all!). If you're going to write studio ideas, you have to assume, nitty-grittywise, that life is absurd. You *do* assume that, don't you? It's all a game. There are altogether too many pompous clowns flapping around who take all this foolishness seriously. This is not to say there aren't serious issues or legitimate causes. Obviously, there are glaring, long-standing wrongs to be righted, but it seems to me that we have an absolute genius for ignoring, or at least fumbling the real problems, and making life and death issues out of whether or not we should have 28¼ rather than 28½ acres of tarmac and neon in any given beautification program. I'm telling you, sweet person, if this society of ours isn't a fountainhead of gag possibilities, I will personally, and without flinching, hand you my rubber duck for keepsies.

Living in these United States makes it that much easier to come up with stuff like this:

COVER: (Hippie type smoking and holding chamber pot
        type of container)
        I just can't keep it to myself any longer . . .
INSIDE: . . . you're the one I'd like to share my pot with . . .

COVER: On your birthday . . . why not try a little
        of that good ol' L.S.D.
INSIDE: *Liquor, Sex,* and *Deviltry!*

COVER: Birthday time rolling around again?
        Look . . . take my advice . . .
INSIDE: . . . DON'T GET INVOLVED!
        Cheers!

    COVER: (Neuter standing in front of Christmas tree)
           In spite of what they say, Christmas is still
           the same as it always was!
    INSIDE: . . and I'll bet my aluminum tree on it!!!
           Happy Holidays!

All of these idea sources I've described, however, offer very few ideas directly. By this, I mean the idea that hits you immediately, and you just know it's a greeting card . . . and a good one.

For instance, the following ideas came like shots out of the blue — at different times, of course — when greeting cards were the last thing on my mind. Zing! There they were. Gifts! No work involved. No doubt they would sell. Neat, clean, fast . . .

> COVER: As you enter the service . . . here's the first
> part of your uniform . . .
> INSIDE: (Olive drab button attachment)
> It's for your lip

> COVER: Granny had a word for birthdays
> INSIDE: The word was "CRAP!"
> Happy Day

I'm conscious of getting only a small percentage of my ideas via thunderbolts, though, 10%, maybe 15%. Who knows, who cares?

Now, let me tell you how I really get 'em. The secret! A working day . . . rise promptly for breakfast and afterwards lie down and get right to work. If you're the athletic type and have something to prove, you can write sitting up, but that doesn't prove anything in particular to me. Gather a few simple tools together . . . dictionary, thesaurus, paper, and a plastic pencil guaranteed to last 30 words or 30 seconds, whichever comes first. Turn loose. Just think gags and relate them to sendable situations. Some secret, huh? Well, if you've done your reading, kept your ears open, been to the card racks and, indeed, do have a sense of humor, something *has* to happen. I usually start slow in the morning by running a few old card ideas through my mind. There are always a few favorite cards, words or phrases that stick with you. This, just to get in first gear. A few variations will develop — strange situations, a popular or hip saying, a couple of words that rhyme, a cute phrase — all of which are atrocious, obvious, and has been done a thousand times by everyone. This might not seem like progress, and maybe it isn't much, but at least it gets the most stagnant thoughts of the day out of the way so as not to waste time with them later. After this remarkable progression will come a handful or two of slightly more original ideas, mostly bad, with the beginnings of a few definite possibilities. During the early afternoon, usually a couple of dozen partially-developed ideas are bouncing around and maybe ten or twelve definites are put on ice. I'll add a few new possibilities, rewrite some of the previous ones, and during the last part of the afternoon everything, somehow, starts falling into place and completed ideas will come in clusters. At the end of a full day, there should be between forty and fifty intact ideas. I read them all over immediately and chop out about a half dozen of the very worst, not throwing them away, however, because even from this compost heap something can occasionally be salvaged. The next morning, I read the whole batch through again. Opinions of more than a few will definitely change during the night! Maybe a dozen more ideas will be eliminated. So, I will have thirty or so ideas to show for the previous day's work. If I'm not working on a definite assignment with a specific deadline, I put these ideas away for a week or two before reading them over once again. The last check-over! It's easy to overdo this reviewing business, and there is a tendency to rewrite the very life out of an idea if you look at it long enough. When working to a deadline, I make the choices more quickly, which, when you've built up a little experience, isn't much of a gamble. You learn over the years that when certain types of ideas have been rejected by every card manufacturer in the world time and time again, chances are that this wasn't such a hot approach after all. I would advise the new writer, though, to let those hot ideas and that simmering head cool off for a few days before making the final decisions. I guarantee that you will be horror stricken with some of your creations. I still suffer from an uncontrollable twitching in the presence of my ever-mounting supply of rejects. The ones that have come home to die. Pure twaddle. I've done evrything wrong there is to do, and I continue to do it on a certain percentage of cards. Look, they can't all be jewels. We do the best we can, Pal, and that's it! The objective is not to waste the editor's time with *all* your worst efforts. Remember, they have their own exclusive hang-ups to untangle, and have only so much time to devote to you personally and greeting cards in general.

On a writing day, then, I shoot for thirty or forty ideas. If they're Everyday ideas, about 60-65% will eventually make it to print. For certain Seasonal stuff, like Christmas ideas, the percentage will be lower. All of these ideas certainly won't be sold in the highest-priced markets during the first two weeks! It may take quite a while but remember, sitting under some pert secretary, somewhere, is an editor or publisher with a fat wallet and a printing deadline of his own to meet. If you give him an honest effort, like his secretary does, your chances are pretty good . . . maybe better . . . *she* might be frigid.

I'm sure there are some hot hands that would pshaw at thirty or forty ideas per day as a goal. They really crank them out! But quantity is not the name of the game. What's the sense of turning them out if they don't stand some small chance? I couldn't even come up with thirty or forty ideas a day, five days a week, week after week. It could de done for a while but things just have to get stale after a bit. Ask any horse.

Fortunately, you will not have to sustain your creative energies fulltime. When you have a few hundred ideas going, you will spend more than a little time keeping records of where they are, who has bought what, who needs what, and when. If you're inefficient, which you'll remember was a prerequisite, you will never have enough stamps or envelopes, and the typewriter ribbon will always be in sideways. When you get a few thousand ideas going, confusion escalates. Naturally, you will also spend three or four days a month just hauling sacks of money to the bank. All of these little time-consumers are part of running a small business and, although boring, they at least make you eager to get back to writing — and that's the way you should come to it. Even when you pace your writing, you'll turn out lemons. It is unavoidable. Don't worry about them. There are marginal ideas you're not quite sure of, you're just about positive that they're bad, but there's a lingering doubt. So, you send them off. Gag writers, like pols and general staffs, once they have set an idea in motion find it difficult to rein back, even if it stinks.

Another little involvement that can eat up hours is artwork. This can work to your advantage or disadvantage, depending on how proficient you are at drawing or sketching. If you honestly feel you have no talent in this area, just type out your ideas plain. If they're good, they'll sell in this form. After all, this is what it's all about — ideas! If, however, you like to sketch little comic figures, or the neuter, blob-type characters you see on so many studio cards, and can do it quickly, fine. It can't hurt. This type of artwork will not turn a bad idea into a good one, but it can put any idea into a more impressive package. What value this has, everything else being equal, is debatable. It's up to you. However, if you decide to use simple illustrations, study those little characters when you go out to look over cards. At first glance, they appear very elementary, and a great many are neuter, sex-wise, but look closely at those facial expressions, body positions, gestures of arms, legs, shoulders, eyelids, mouth, fingers, etc. These little figures are happy, or sad, or confused, or angelic, or bitter, or excited, or fatigued, or serene, or just about anything depending on the gist of the idea. They back up the idea. They're in harmony with it. For example:

If you can't quickly sketch the right expression or gesture but, on the contrary, consistently turn out vapid, lifeless characters, or worse yet, characters with the wrong expressions, they can only fight the ideas, not help them. However, at this point in the development of a card, the artwork is just not that important. Don't get hung up on it.

Don't Get Discouraged — Part II. Rejection slips! PHHHhhht! I have mine made into suits and what's left over, sell to paper junkies at a nickel a ton. These slips read, in spite of the fact that they're not intended to, like the final death blow. They're not as cold as they look. Editors simply don't have time to write consoling, explanatory little notes. Find a good tailor or dressmaker.

Don't Get Discouraged — Part III. Almost all editors have certain types of ideas they do not want to see, but what is not wanted varies from editor to editor. No sex stuff, please! No bedpan or belly button gags! No topical ideas! No hip jargon! No brand names! Nothing too cutsie-pie. No ficticious personal names! No trick folds! No whatever! You may wonder occasionally if there is anything left. Well, if you can relate it to a sendable situation and get it to the *right company,* you can sell it! Different companies have an image to maintain or protect or, for one reason or another they have found that certain types of ideas just do not sell in their particular line. They know what they're doing. (Except, of course, the ones who have folded in the past few years. Hoo-ha!) If an editor states he doesn't want to see a particular type of idea, don't keep throwing it in his face, or give him advice about his unimaginative approach to publishing. They have their different markets and they know as well as anyone what sells in them. Occasionally, you can slip in a taboo subject or two, just to see if anyone is paying attention. Companies have been known, on rare occasions, to change their editorial viewpoints. As a free-lancer, you've got to keep probing. Just don't push too hard. You will quickly learn that each company has a distinct personality of its own and that if you channel the right idea to the right company, very few subjects or approaches are forbidden.

For instance, here are a few studio ideas that *had* to go to the right type of company. It would have been a waste of everyone's time to send them out indiscriminately.

> COVER: (Rear view of woman in topless bathing suit)
> When it comes to these daring new one-piece bathing suits . . .
> INSIDE: I will if you will!
> (Card folds out to reveal man wearing only bra walking hand in hand with woman on cover)

(To take advantage of topical material such as the topless bathing suit was at one point, a card company occasionally has to get the idea and artwork through the presses and distributed on the retail racks in a very short time. As a gag writer, you have to be able to move in order to hold up your end of it. Also, you have to find out which companies encourage this type of idea and are geared to follow through with it.)

> COVER: Happy Mother's Day, Mom dear . . . and although I don't usually talk this way, I want you to know I think you're . . .
> INSIDE: . . . one helluva nice MOTHER!

(The word is "helluva" and it's the basis for the whole idea, but there are a few companies that wouldn't touch this type of thing . . . even though it would have to be classified as a "cute" idea.)

A word about integrity. I know you're honest, but you worry about some of those big companies and what they do with your precious, unprotected ideas, right? The honesty of the companies, as well as yourself, should be dictated, if not by sheer morality, at least by common sense. They are *not* going to make copies of your ideas or artwork and return the originals to you with a rejection slip. If you feed them junk, they wouldn't want to steal it even if they were bandits. If you're valuable to them as a contributor, they want to keep you happy. Trust them! Trust me! They play a perfectly honest game of ball, both the large and small companies! The checks are good and usually quite prompt. In return, you don't play hanky-panky with ideas, naturally. The editors and their cohorts who check over your ideas know pretty much what this game is all about. They have a built-in sensitivity to most ideas that have been used before, in their particular line as well as other lines. As mentioned before, borrowing an idea from a source other than greeting cards and converting it to a card situation is not exactly plagiarism, you understand, but borrowing something from another greeting card without giving it something original of your own is something else again. Use some old-fashioned common sense. If something looks at all like trouble, drop it quick. Get on to something positive.

The future of studio cards, along with the future of greeting cards in general, looks good, but why, I'll never know. I suppose it is simply easier to send words written and printed by someone else than it is to sit down and write a note personally. After all, if you can't communicate orally, or for some reason choose not to, it would seem that a handwritten note would be a more sincere way to do it. So, who has the time or the talent to do things right? A few still do, I'm told, but not many. So, we have greeting cards, and in my world they fall into two categories — *studios* and *others* — and the *others* don't make it. I'm talking about cards for adults, now. Juvenile cards are in a class by themselves. To some extent, I represent the fans who have grown up with studios and there are more followers coming along all the time.

The sweet, lengthy verses of the *others* are simply a bit much. To be sure, they make up the greater part of the industry today — probably will forever — and, obviously, they have their legions who lap them up, but to each his own, Hirschel. The pack I run with simply feel that for someone else to state our feelings of concern in the form of a sweet little poem — not to be confused with poetry — for us to buy and send is all a bit slick. On the other hand, we won't write those intimate little notes, either. We settle for studio cards. It's a cop-out to the personal touch but you can live with it. It's a less traditional, less pretentious way of saying the same old things. This doesn't mean we have to be sarcastic, irreverent, or risque, although we can be. We can also be cute, sweet, whimsical, just plain nice, without making a production out of it. Studios are like the people who enjoy sending and receiving them, the young and those who think young (or thing they do, anyhow). A little more direct, uncluttered and candid, but not way, way out or completely demented — like so:

COVER: Another birthday!?
INSIDE: Well, bless your brittle little bones . . .
            Happy Day!!!

COVER: On your birthday . . . no ill-conceived remarks
            about candle-laden cakes, or inebriated
            celebrations, or midriff expansion or such;
            just a simple wish I hope you'll find
            refreshing.
INSIDE: May your cesspool never clog.

COVER: If you think you've got troubles, cheer up . . .
INSIDE: Auntie Gertrude's living bra dropped dead
            right on *MAIN STREET!!!*
            Get well soon!

COVER: Happy Anniversary . . . eat, drink and be merry . . .
INSIDE: . . . for tomorrow you may be with child . . .

To wind it up then. Don't make a fetish out of looking for formulas to follow and rules to remember that will guarantee the perfect ideas every time. Let the editors do the heavy worrying about such matters. They're better at it than we are. Part of their job, after all, is to make those final, nasty, tight decisions. Our job is to give them as wide and effective a choice as possible. As idea people, we're in at the very beginning of a greeting card, and this is no time to pussyfoot. Unwind! Throw a few curves! Zingers! Tempered, of course, and, ahem, with a little bit of common sense, restraint and self-editing. But not too much.

Remember, you're not a machine, you're *you*. No one else! Big deal, you say? Well, some people tend to forget this. They try to wear the bag the way others have worn it before. Come on now, that's not going to do it, you know that! For those *original* ideas, it comes back to you alone. *Your* viewpoints. It's really the only thing you've got going for you.

If you decide to give it a go, I'll tell you the *real* story when we meet in person, maybe at the post office, as you send off a batch of money-makers. You'll recognize me. I'll be the one standing out front on the sidewalk — wrapped in a horse blanket. Selling used plastic pencils.

Chapter XI

My Secrets of Writing Studio Cards... or In the Heat of the Night

by Johnnie Wolfe

The editor of this potpourri sashayed up to me sidesaddle the other day and tried to convince me that out there in the real world are literally hundreds, Yea! thousands, of hopeful studio card writers waiting for me to share all my secrets on how I write hilarious studio greeting cards. Since I convince easily (Someone once convinced me to sell my Edsel stock and buy Cuban coffee), I have decided to fulfill you by revealing my all — and also tell you how I write studio cards.

The first thing you might wonder is *where do I get my ideas?* Well, some of them I get standing on a street corner on a windy day — but the kind you're interested in I get from several places:

Books Collections of jokes, comedy bits, limericks, one-liners, combos, etc. Any book that contains humor of any kind, — Art Buchwald's books, Bennett Cerf's books, humorous short story collections, non-fiction books, and novels.

Magazines Cartoons and satire magazines — *Playboy, Reader's Digest, Mad* — and any and all mags that run jokes, cartoons, bits of life, humorous fiction and non-fiction. Even the ads in these magazines can key you to a topical subject or an in-vogue expression.

Television and Radio Television talk programs — Johnny Carson, Joey Bishop, Mer-r-ve — the comedians on *any* program and TV and radio commercials. These are an even better source of current fads and in-vogue jazz than magazines because they hit and affect millions of people at the same time, — the same people (bless their little quarters) your greeting card ideas have to hit.

Cliches Old or new well-known expressions. Slogans or expressions from television and radio commercials and shows if the saying becomes popular enough.

Well-Known Personalities A trait, characteristic, favorite expression, slogan, name, or what-have-you of a famous person, living or dead — and sometimes you can't tell the difference.

Songs Song titles or words from the body of the song. Watch for copyrights.

Cartoon Characters Well-known characters from the daily and Sunday comics or from cartoon shows on television. Usage is about the same as for well-known personalities, but here watch for copyrights; don't be overly worried about them, however, because it's the editor's job to handle copyright problems. You provide the ideas, not the legal smeltz.

Jokes Jokes you hear that may never be written down. Like the one about the girl who — but I digress. That's a joke for a different book.

Greeting Cards It is often possible to rewrite the gag from a published card into something better, or write a new gag for an attachment on a published card, or a new gag around a mechanical action that you find on either a studio card or a humorous card. All of these are legal rewrites and switches — so long as you don't simply change a couple of words, or the sequence of words, and try to sell the idea as your own. Besides not being legal or ethical, it's a sure sign of no talent, and you've got enough talent of your own so that you don't have to leech someone else's work.

Those are my sources, or starting points, for getting ideas. I've also tried a few other ones that I've heard of from time to time, and I'll tell you about them as well as about how I get ideas from scratch. But first, maybe you'd like to see some of the studio card ideas I wrote from my sources, and hear how I went about writing them (all are ideas that I sold).

Books   Here is a joke I read in a collection of slightly off-color (*blue, if you want a specific color*) comedy bits. The off-color book, incidentally, is a great source of risque greeting card ideas.

> COMIC: I just heard that along with all the other kinds of records they've got like "Music to Dance By," "Music to Listen To," "Music to Soothe You," they've now got a record you play in your bathroom.
>
> STOOGE: Play in your *bathroom?* What kind of music does the record play?
>
> COMIC: It's called "Music to Move You!"

I took the premise of this gag, "music to move you," and tried to think of what kind of greeting card occasion it would logically fit. At first, I thought of a gift record for a birthday, but the "Music to Move You" had no logical tie-in with a birthday. I finally decided the only occasion it would logically tie-in with would be an illness of some type — but I wasn't too crazy about sending a sick person a record because it isn't normally done. Records have no place in a hospital. So the problem was what to use that could play records or music and had some logical relation to a sick person. Then I remembered recently seeing a bunch of transistor radios in the shape of clocks, spice cabinets, recipe cabinets, and several other odds and ends. Everything fell into place and this is what I came up with:

> Heard you were sick, so I'm sending you the latest medical aid — a bedpan with a built-in transistor radio . . .
>
> . . . it plays music to move you!!!

How much did I get for the idea? $40. The source book for the idea cost me $1.95.

Here's an idea I got out of a book of copyright-free illustrations (see the Bibliography). I cut out a number of illustrations of old guns, large and small, of all types and pasted them on the cover of my card dummy. The text accompanying the illustrations went like so:

> CONGRATULATIONS!!!
> . . . You're going great guns!!

The book of illustrations cost me ten dollars, and I got $50 back for this idea.

Magazines   Here's a card idea I got from an ad featured in both magazines and on television. The ad was for a sugar-free soft drink, and played around the phrase *girl watchers.* The premise of the ad was that if a girl drank the soft drink, she would become so tantalizingly slim that all the *girl watchers* would watch her. For my card idea, I drew a picture (I've had several years of art training, and so can do both rough and finished art work on cards) of a sexy gal on the cover being *watched* by a couple of guys. The text ran:

> Happy Birthday to a girl . . .
> . . . that girl watchers watch!

Television and Radio   I was listening one night to the Merv Griffin Show, and I heard Mer-r-ve crack that old joke, which I had forgotten: *How do porcupines make love? . . . Very carefully!* The minute I heard the joke, I associated it, for some unknown reason (which I guess some would say was my writer's subconscious working), with a song title: *I Love You So Much It Hurts.* I jotted the whole thing down in my ever-present notebook and later tied it all together into this card idea:

> Valentine, as one porcupine said to the other
> . . . "I love you so much it hurts!"

Song titles, as this card illustrates, can often be switched into card ideas.

Clichés   To demonstrate the uses of clichés, here's a long text card in which I used every related cliché I could think of. The idea started while I was going over a long list of clichés I've collected over the years. I noticed a relationship between a couple of the clichés, so I went through the list for more and came up with a whole list of related ones. I tied them to a logical greeting card occasion, and this is the way they came out:

(This idea was illustrated with various shapes and sizes of fish.)

> HOLY MACKERAL!!! You having a birthday?!? Well, don't FLOUNDER around like a poor SOLE — Just for the HALI-BUT go out and PERCH on a bar stool and have a WHALE of a time — you'd be a SUCKER not to, even if it costs you a couple of FINS! (Could there be something FISHY about this card??) You're CLAM right!!!

Well-Known Personalities   Here's one way — and there are many others — that I've used well-known personalities in a greeting card:

> Someone asked me if you ever knocked a few years off your age???
> ... And I said: Did Babe Ruth hit home runs?
> Does Garbo want to be alone?
> Did Benjamin Franklin fly a kite?

Cartoon Characters   There are two things to watch out for when using cartoon characters in your gags. If your character is the popular-now-but-maybe-not-tomorrow-type, be certain you get your ideas into the editor in a hurry. The ideas would be classified as topical humor, and the card company would need them while the character's popularity was still on the way up, not on the way down. When you see a cartoon character begin-ning to make a splash, get your stuff in!

The other type of character to use is the old faithful, very-well known, been-around-for-years-character. In most cases, these old-time characters have been tied up in copyrights for years. You waste time writing an idea using them directly because it's either impossible, or not worth it, to get greeting card rights and pay royalties for the character. Your best bet with these characters is to satirize them, write something near enough to them so that they can be easily recognized. For example, guess who I got this character from:

> What is that racing across the sky with a
> belated birthday message??? It's a bird!!!
> It's a plane!!! . . .
> . . . It's SUPERGOOF!!!
> (Sorry! Hope your day was happy!)

Jokes   Listen to the jokes your children tell you, your friends tell you, your boss tells you, even those your husband or wife tells you. But *now* listen to them with the thought of switching them somehow into greeting card ideas. You'll find you'll laugh louder at the joke if you suddenly switch it in your mind and get that tickling feeling that it may be a $50 number. There's another chapter in this book that tells you how to switch anything your heart desires, so I won't go into the mechanics. Just keep in mind that there is a card idea in nearly every joke you hear if you can just look at it and slant it the right way. Here are a couple I've done — original joke, and the greeting card idea:

> A man in a restaurant ordered a bowl of soup,
> The waiter brought it and put it on the table.
> The man took one look at it and called to the waiter,
> "Waiter, what is this fly doing in my soup?"
> The waiter bent over, looked into the soup, and
> then said, "I think it's the backstroke, Sir."

Before I give you the card idea, I wrote from this joke, let me digress for a moment and mention that the punchline on this joke is a great one on which to practice switches, as is the entire joke. Why not try some just for practice?

Here's the card idea I wrote:

> For your birthday I bought you a nice birthday
> cake . . . but to my dismay I found a fly in it . . .
> (Inside I drew a character holding a cake in
> one hand and a zipper in the other. The text read:)
> . . . which is darned unusual!!!

Greeting Cards Published cards are an excellent source to key off new ideas. They already contain all the essential greeting card ingredients, and so serve as good examples of what your idea must contain: me-to-you message, lots of you's, etc. They also provide you with things to write about, like bedpans, hypodermic needles, sponges, sand paper, candles, etc. Published greeting cards give you the benefit of the training, experience, and knowledge of free-lance writers, staff writers, designers, editors, art directors, and artists from all over the country, and some of the city.

Warning! Be careful when using published cards to key off ideas, there is always a tendency to write ideas too close to the card you are using. There is no set rule-of-the-middle-finger on how close is too close. Only experience can teach you this. But in the beginning, you are better off being over-cautious. If you write an idea that you think might be too close to the published card, file the idea away until you get enough experience to judge it better. Sending around a batch of ideas that are too close to published cards could mar your reputation, so use this rule when submitting ideas: If in doubt, leave it out! End of lecture.

Now here's an idea I wrote, from a Christmas card that said, *At Christmas, you wanna know how to make a reindeer fly? . . . First you get a zipper about 12 inches long . . .*

I used the fly/zipper play on words and came up with this birthday gag for a $1.00 card. (Those are the giant-size kind.)

> As a special treat on your birthday, ya wanna see
> an elephant fly??? . . .
> (On the inside, I drew a picture of a humorous
> elephant standing up straight, human bean style,
> and wearing over-sized pants. On the front of the
> pants I glued an actual zipper about six inches
> long that I bought at a department store.)

How much did I get for the idea? $70. How much did I pay for the zipper? 29¢. Shameful, isn't it?! (Ed. note: Agreed! Especially since I'm the one who bought that idea from Johnnie. The card outsold any other dollar card in our line for almost six months!)

Ideas from Scratch These are the ideas you get from that thing you carry around with you all the time: your head. They come from an accumulation of the things you see, read, hear, do, think, feel, want — anything and everything that you've ever experienced in your life, or haven't experienced yet but want to. The trick is to get your mind working and using all those things so you can get something salable down on paper. Here are some of the techniques I use to get myself going.

Play-on-Words I try to think of all the words that sound alike but have different meanings, words with double meaning, slang words, clichés that can be changed in meaning by changing a word or two or the order of the words, and any trick that can be done with words. I throw the words together, look at them sideways, from the top, bottom, left side, right side, every possible way I can. There is no special way of doing this, you just have to let your imagination roam wild. Here are a couple of ideas I dug up this way. Remember the elephant-fly gag? That's a play-on-words, right?!)

> Without you at Easter . . .
> (illustration of very sad bunny) . . . my
> hoppiness is gone!

> (Illustration of sad farmer and cow on cover)
> I forgot your birthday . . . and to make matters worse,
> my cow went dry . . .
> . . . talk about udder failure!

Lead-Ins In this technique, I try to think of as many standard lead-ins to greeting card gags as I can; for example, here are a few common Get Well lead-ins:

> Heard your doctor is world famous for . . .
> Just heard your doctor called in a specialist to . . .
> Don't worry about your operation, you've got a great
>   doctor . . . he once operated on . . .
> Your doctor wants to give you some unusual tests . . .
> Sorry you're sick, let me know if there is anything
>   I can do, like . . .

One type of Get Well gag I always try to write is a *Belly Button gag*. Why, you ask? I've been waiting to tell you.

When I was a greeting card editor, one writer used to send me dozens of gags that had something or other to do with belly buttons, most of them hilarious. I finally nicknamed him *The Belly Button King.* During one period, I nearly went into a thing trying to write better belly button gags than he did. I used to sit around like Buddha and contemplate my navel and try to do any funny thing with it that I could work into a greeting card. Don't laugh! Here's one I came up with:

> Don't worry about your operation . . . you've
> got a great doctor . . . he once operated on my
> uncle and it was a complete success except for
> one small side effect . . .
> . . . everytime my uncle raises his arm his belly
> button puckers!

Here are some Friendship and Birthday lead-ins:

> They don't come any nicer than you . . .
> Just the thought of you makes me . . .

> I like you, you're . . .
> Since you've been gone, I've been . . .
> Birthdays shouldn't worry you, you've . . .
> You may be older, but . . .

Once I get a couple of these lead-ins, I start digging for something to go with them. For example:

> They don't come any nicer than you . . .
> Younger maybe, but not nicer!
> Since you've been gone, I've been going out a lot,
> dancing a lot, laughing a lot . . .
> . . . lying a lot!! (I miss you)

Related Subjects   I try to think of all the things, like special knowledge, that are related to a particular subject. For example, to do some service cards recently, I started thinking of all the silly things they use to make us sing while marching in basic training — things like *G.I. Beans, G.I. Gravy, G.I. Wish I Had Joined the Navy!* This is the only printable one I can remember. From this one and others, I came up with this card idea:

> (On the cover I drew a girl dreaming about a
> serviceman.)
> G.I. Brave, G.I. True . . .
> . . . G.I. wish I wuz with you!

I guess the idea expressed what a lot of girls wanted to say because it became a fairly good seller (Ed. note: It was bought by the Barker Greeting Card Company and is still their #1 selling Serviceman's card.)

Right here, I'd like to stop and get sloppy for a sec. Besides the money you can make writing greeting cards, it's kind of a great feeling to know that you're helping people to communicate with each other, to express emotions that they can't find the words to express; that the people who receive the cards you write may turn on, rejoice, guffaw, snicker, do back flips, break up, get tickled, slap their thighs, smile, and maybe even feel better. Some of the biggest kicks I get come from watching people in a card shop pick up a card I wrote and laugh over it and hurriedly show it to a friend so they can laugh too, and then buy it so they can share the humor and emotion with someone else, perhaps a husband or wife or lover or relative or friend. It makes me glad I've got this talent, and it makes all the long hours I've spent developing it and using it worthwhile. End of sentimental jazz.

As I mentioned at the beginning of this opus, I'm always looking for new ways to get ideas, so when I heard a while back of one writer who gets ideas in a bathtub, I decided to give it a try. I filled my tub with hot water, tossed in some weird things the writer recommended, and gingerly stepped in. As I did, I had the strangest feeling that I was finally getting my feet wet in the greeting card business. I lay back in the water, and immediately ideas ran hot and cold through me. They came so fast and furious, I had the feeling I was suddenly being showered with them — but then I realized that my foot had hit the shower faucet and turned it on. Nevertheless, I knew that if I could just find some way to wash the ideas out of my mind, I was bound to have a lot of them that would sell, even if a few of them were all wet and went down the drain. Finally, as I sat there in all my glory, a greeting card writer at work, an idea came leaking through to me. Here it is:

> Valentine, here's how a couple of people, like us,
> can have some good, clean fun on Valentine's Day . . .
> . . . (Inside I drew an illustration of a couple
> in a bathtub.)

Altogether, it was a refreshing and revealing experience, but there is one thing I found wrong with writing in the bathtub — it ruined the ribbon on my typewriter.

My last secret may not be a secret at all but more a method or personal temperament. I work very late at night, when it's dark and quiet outside and there are no ringing phones or well-meaning visitors to bother me. Sometimes 3 o'clock in the morning will find me still bending heatedly over my desk or drawing board. Working late at night has another advantage for me. I sleep until noon and don't start work until about 8 o'clock at night, so this leaves me the entire afternoon to browse through card stores, the library, department stores, book stores, and all the other dozens of places you might find card ideas. The point is that no matter what hours you write, you should always schedule some time for research and refreshing yourself mentally. The walking around and looking bit may at first give you the feeling that you're not doing anything, but ignore it. It's worth its time in money.

Well, there's my all — my writing secrets too. Now that I've shared myself with you, how about *you* sharing yourself with me?! If you've got any writing secrets then send them to me! After all, in this business we're all brothers under the skin — or *sisters.*

Chapter XII

Things to Be Funny About

by H. Joseph Chadwick

Now that you've learned *how* to write funny cards, it's time to learn *what* to be funny about. To do this, let's see how a greeting card company might break down its studio and humorous cards.

First, they would separate them into two general lines of cards: *Everyday* cards and *Seasonal* cards. Everyday cards are those that are sent everyday of the year. These are *birthday, get well, anniversary*, and *friendship* cards. Seasonal cards are those cards that are sent only during the several holidays and special days we observe. These are *New Year's, Valentine's Day, St. Patrick's Day, Easter, April Fool's Day, Mother's Day, Father's Day, Graduation, Sweetest Day, Halloween, Thanksgiving, Hannakuh, Jewish New Year, Thanksgiving,* and *Christmas.* Not all companies publish cards for each of these days. Some publish cards for all the days, while others publish cards for none. Always ask the editors what seasonal cards they publish and when before submitting seasonal ideas to them.

Now that we have our two lines established, let's take a detailed look at the Everyday line. The Everyday line is broken down into four *categories:* birthday, get well, anniversary, and friendship. The cards within these categories are then separated into *captions.* Since the birthday cards are the most important ones — half of all the cards sold in the everyday line are birthday cards — let's study that one first.

A *caption* shows who the card will be sent to. Thus, a *female* caption means that the card must be written so it can be sent to a woman; a *male* caption means it must be written so it can be sent to a man; an *Uncle* caption means it can be sent to an uncle, and so on. Here are a few ideas written for specific captions:

BELATED BIRTHDAY CAPTION:
> Forgetting your birthday really
> burns me up . . .
> . . . In fact, I feel like an ash!

WIFE CHRISTMAS CAPTION:
> Who needs Santa Claus when I've
> got a wife like you . . .
> . . . you've got all the goodies!

The birthday caption you'll be writing for most is the *general* caption. For this caption, the ideas are written so that the card can be sent to anyone by anyone. For example:

> For your birthday, I didn't know whether you
> would want money or a card . . .
> . . . so I took a chance with a card!

As you can see, this card could be bought by either sex and sent to either sex, regardless of their relationship, so the *general* caption obviously gives a card the greatest possible range of buyers. And that is why it is used so much in all categories. So, remember, write most of your birthday ideas for the general caption.

Here is a list of commonly used birthday captions that are often asked for by editors. Write about half of your gags for the *general* caption, but occasionally write gags for the other captions to give variety to your submissions and because editors will be asking for them.

General	Sweet Sixteen	Dad
Male	Boy Teenager	Wife
Teenager	Sports . . . usually	Relative
Girl Teenager	broken down into bowling,	Brother
21st Birthday	fishing, golf, and general	Mother
Belated Birthday	sports.	Sister
Female	From Group	Husband
Jewish	*From* both of us	Serviceman

After the birthday category, the next most important one is the *friendship* category. One reason for its place of importance is that it consists of cards that cover *all* the sending situations that do not fall into the *birthday, get well,* and *anniversary* categories.

Generally, the most important friendship caption is *missing you,* followed closely — and sometimes surpassed — by the *general* caption. (The *missing you* caption varies radically in popularity depending on whether or not we're in a war, as do the *In Service* and *Entering Service* captions. By comparison, the *general* caption stays in a relatively steady state.)

Here are the commonly used *friendship* captions:

General	Wedding	Dieting
New Home	Thank you	Promotion
Trip	Birth — boy	Congratulations
Thinking of you	Birth	Entering service
Congratulations . . .	Missing you	Bar Mitzvah
from group	Write	Birth — girl
Retirement	New Apartment	Returning from service
New Car	Vacation	Goodbye
In Service		

The third most important category is *get well.* With the advent of Medicare and increased longevity, this category is becoming stronger almost daily. It is doubtful that it will ever surpass either the *birthday* or *friendship* categories, but it does possess a much more important position in greeting cards than it ever has in the past.

Here are the commonly used captions in the *get well* category:

General	Operation	Hospital
Male	Female	Accident
From group	Jewish	

The final category in the *everyday* cards is the *anniversary* category. Although this category automatically brings to mind wedding anniversaries, remember that some people celebrate, or at least remember, other types of anniversaries, such as job, house, business, going steady, or anything and everything that can possibly have an anniversary. For this reason, write some of your *general* anniversary ideas to cover any type of anniversary occasion. For example:

> There is only *one thing* to say about your
> anniversary . . .
> CONGRATULATIONS!

But, regardless of the many types of anniversaries there are, the most popular one is and always will be the marriage anniversary. So write 95 percent of your anniversary ideas for this one caption alone.

Here is a list of popular marriage anniversary captions:

General	Wife	Our
To both	Better half	Mom and Dad
Belated	Jewish	Husband

Now that we've covered the four *everyday* categories, and the captions within these categories and we have a fairly good idea of who we'll be writing the cards for — i.e., someone who has had an operation, or an accident, or is going into the service, or a girl having a birthday, etc. — let's study some of the things, or themes, we can write about.

Since the most popular caption in the birthday category is the *general* caption, let's take a look at some of the themes that we might use in this caption.

One of the often used birthday themes is the *celebrate* one. Using this theme, we write our ideas to either tell the card receiver to live it up on his birthday, or imply that he's going to have a wing-ding of a celebration. We can even throw ourselves into the theme by suggesting that we be invited to help the person celebrate. Here are a few examples of this theme:

> It's your birthday, so live it up! . . .
> . . . while you're still young enough to live it down!

> To help celebrate your birthday this year I wanted
> to send you something special to hold your booze . . .
> . . . so here I am!!!

Another popular birthday theme is one based on *sports.* For example:

> Happy Birthday to the world's greatest sports
> lover . . .
> . . . indoors and out!

Still another birthday theme that stays high in popularity, especially with people who don't send gifts, is the *poverty* theme. Here's one:

> Sorry I couldn't send you a few bucks in this
> birthday card, but I'm broke . . .
> . . . what are you looking in here for, I told
> you I'm broke!!!

Now let's jump over into the *friendship* category and take a look at a few examples of themes used in the *general* and *missing you* captions.

This first theme is based on *giving a compliment.* It will probably give you more sales than any other theme. Like this one:

I like you . . .
. . . you're nicer than warm sheets in
January!

Now you've got to admit that there is something extra-special about that idea. So give lots of thought to the *complimentary* theme . . . if you can come up with some good ones, they're bound to sell. Here is one:

Happiness is . . .
. . . having a friend like you!

Here are a few *general* ideas from the *get well* category. One of the most popular themes for get wells is the *suggestive* theme, especially when *body humor* is used. Here's one:

(Character in bed with thermometer in mouth)
You think you're sick now, huh?? . . .
. . . wait until you hear where your thermometer's
been!

The *suggestive* theme, using sex humor, is also highly popular in the *anniversary* category when it is used for a *wedding* anniversary. Here is an example:

If you two are just going to celebrate your
anniversary like everyone else . . .
. . . you might as well go back to bed!

Now that you've gotten the idea of what a theme is, here is a list of some of the more popular themes used in the *everyday* categories. Examples of published gags using the particular theme are also given.

Birthday Themes

Suggestive: This is a strong theme, especially when sex humor is used.

For your birthday, here's the secret of how to
improve your sex life . . .
. . . practice, practice!

Sex humor is especially good when writing gags for a *male* caption.

Gift Gag: This has many sub-themes, such as *Wanted to get you a gift but:*

> Had a great gift all picked out for your birthday,
> but I couldn't lift it . . .
> . . . the saleslady was watching me!

Or, *Got you a gift but:*

> Misery is buying a fifth of imported scotch
> for someone's birthday and having it slip out
> of your hands while you're wrapping it and then
> trying to clean it all up off the floor . . .
> . . . and getting a tongue full of splinters!

Or. *Tried to get you a gift but:*

> Walked all over town looking for a birthday
> present for you and guess what I almost got?? . . .
> . . . arrested for street walking!

Or, *The sender is the gift:*

> For your birthday, I'm sending you something
> that will stand in the corner and hold your
> entire liquor supply . . .
> . . . ME!!!

Or, *The gift is in the card:*

> Here's a little something that will really
> tickle your fancy . . .
> . . . (feather attachment)

There are many more sub-themes in the *gift gag* theme. Study the cards on the racks to see the many ways this one theme is used. When you find what seems to be a new way, write up a short specification for it, along with the gag you found, and try it. It may fit in perfectly with some ideas you've been kicking around but haven't been able to work out.

Age Angle: During the early days of studio cards, this theme was one of the strongest ones around, but it appears to be less popular as time flies by, probably because of our increasing concern with staying young. Like any theme, however, if the gag is funny enough, it will sell. But, remember, the more unpopular the theme, the funnier the gag has to be. Here's an age angle gag that is well handled and would probably not offend even the most age conscious person:

> There's one thing you can say about people
> who lie about their age . . .
> . . . there are a lot of us!

Notice in this idea how the age angle is softened by the sender being included in the gag. Now here is one in which the sender is not included, but that is still handled well enough so that no one should be offended:

> You've come to that time of life when you
> have to make a decision . . .
> . . . either a bigger cake or fewer candles!

Remember, the idea in age angle gags is to *kid* the person about their age, not imply that they are getting old and feeble. Be kind to us elders. Someday you too will be one!

Complimentary: This theme implies that even though the person is growing older, he still looks or acts young:

> Happy Birthday to someone who is old enough to
> know the score . . .
> . . . and young enough to play the game!

It may also simply compliment or say something nice about the receiver:

> Here's hoping your birthday is delightful,
> lively, and full of fun! . . .
> . . . just like you!

Joke: This is a somewhat difficult and often weak theme because it depends strictly upon a joke that is at best loosely tied to the birthday:

> Wanted to send you a full-length mink coat for
> your birthday, so I crossed a mink with a
> gorilla . . . but it didn't work out . . .
> . . . the sleeves were too long!

Regardless of the weakness of this theme, it's worth a try once in a while because with it many a good joke can be turned into a salable card idea. Remember though, the gag *must* be tied somehow to the birthday.

Birthday Angle: This theme plays upon the birthday itself . . . often worked around the idea of birthdays being distasteful or wanting to ignore or forget them:

> I know it's your birthday, but take my advice . . .
> . . . don't get involved!

You'll also see this theme using the opening *A birthday is like:*

> (Sexy girl illustrated) A birthday is like a
> sweater . . .
> . . . it's what you put into it that counts!

Topical: This is an excellent theme, and has the greatest potential for generating best-selling cards. But it must be worked around subjects that are nationally known and almost constantly in the news — such as new fashions, TV commercials that use the same phrase over and over, political figures like the President, or political slogans like *The Great Society.* In addition, the subject must be one that is going to have some staying power, and the cards must be on the racks before the subject is past its peak. Therefore, try to judge your topical subjects and hit the editors with your ideas *before* the peak of popularity is reached. One important reason for this is that most topical cards have a relatively short, but fruitful, life and only last as long as the subject is in the news. Since most card companies work a year to two years ahead of publication date, it will take them from three to six months to work topical cards into their production schedule. Many companies will not buy a good topical gag if they feel the popularity of the subject is almost over, because if it is, it will be completely over by the time the card hits the racks. For this very reason, some card companies will not buy topical cards at all, choosing to lose the extra sales from such cards rather than take a chance on being stuck with a lot of cards they can't sell. So, again, get your topical gags to the editors early. This can't be stressed too much . . . being late with them will undoubtedly cost you sales. Now here are some topical cards that were excellent sellers. This first one was a birthday card based on a soft drink company's slogan:

> It's your birthday, so COME ALIVE! . . .
> . . . you're in the SEXY GENERATION!

And this one was based on the mini-skirt craze:

> For your birthday, here's the very latest
> "in" thing . . .
> . . . a mini-card! (small card attachment)

Watch for fads and things that are repeated nationally over and over. They could be money in your pocket.

Friendship Themes

Love: This is by far the strongest friendship theme, and it will, by nature, become increasingly stronger as more young people buy cards. In this theme, the words *I love you* are either used directly:

> Wanna know how much I love you? . . .
> . . . THIS MUCH! (mechanical arms open out wide
> in childlike gesture)

or the affection is implied:

> (On cover, vari-vue heart illustrated so it
> appears to be pounding wildly out of control) . . .
> . . . (character with heart illustrated inside) I
> can't help it, the little devil does that every
> time I think of you!

Missing You: Cards written around this theme are for persons who are away from each other for various reasons. Since either person can be the one who is *away,* try not to write gags that say something like *since you've been gone,* even though this approach is often used for *In Service* cards. The *missing you* theme is especially strong during a war, but is also becoming more popular due to the increasing mobility of our population. Here's an example:

> I miss you in the wee small hours of the night . . .
> . . . and in the big fat hours of the day!

Complimentary: This theme seems to find its greatest use among the dating crowd. In general, it should be slanted with the opposite sex in mind. But don't forget compliments between friends, also . . . especially women, since they tend to compliment each other more than men do . . . probably because they have more to compliment each other about.

> A pussycat like you . . .
> . . . can cross my path anytime!

Joke: Joke gags seem to go fairly well in the *friendship* category if the gag can be worked with a bit of humorous philosophy or advice:

> Don't put off until tomorrow what you can
> do today . . .
> . . . you may like it and then you can do it
> again tomorrow! WHEE!!!

It also works well with just plain wild jokes kidding about the person who gets the card:

> People keep asking me what I see in you . . . and
> I keep saying . . .
> . . "Go to hell, people!"

Suggestive: Suggestive gags go well in the *friendship* category . . . as they do in all the other categories. And though suggestive humor should ordinarily be handled with restraint, it would be foolish not to admit that extremely risque gags do sell to some companies. How risque the gags can be is something you will have to learn by experience. But, remember, the more risque the gag is, the funnier it has to be to sell, and the available market for highly risque gags is very small. If you have a hilarious risque gag that seems to fit a category perfectly, send it out to the markets that request risque humor, but be careful not to offend those that do not want or like this type of humor. *Be sure of your markets before you mail them highly risque gags!* Now here are some mildly suggestive gags:

> You're nice . . .
> . . . oversexed, but nice!
> You've made me happy . . .
> . . . immoral, but happy!

Topical: Topical humor works well in friendship cards also, and all the things regarding timeliness that were mentioned in the birthday theme section apply here as well. The following friendship gag was based on a cigarette commercial:

> You're the GREATEST, the most SATISFYING, the
> COOLEST, in fact . . .
> . . . I'd rather fight than switch!!!

Get Well Themes

Complimentary: This is a very popular theme, and always

salable. It basically states that even though the receiver is sick, he still looks great. Or he's always looked great and a little thing like an illness sure isn't going to change that. Or it's a darn shame that an illness had to happen to someone as nice as him. Compliments are particularly effective when written for a woman, just as they are when spoken for a woman. Here are two of the written ones:

> Illnesses happen to the nicest people . . .
> . . . guess that's why this one happened to you.

> Hope they don't give you any of those wonder drugs . . .
> . . . you're wonderful enough as it is.

Suggestive: As previously mentioned, the best suggestive humor in the *get well* category seems to be the body humor type; but, naturally, sex humor also finds its way into get well cards. Here's one:

> Are you going to get out of that bed? . .
> . . . or am I going to have to come in after you?!?

Doctors: Hundreds of *get well* cards have been written around doctors, and hundreds more will be written in the future, so it's always a good salable theme to try. One point: doctor cards seem to sell much better than those about nurses, except for suggestive *male get well* cards. This is probably because nurses are ordinarily confined to hospitals while doctors attend patients both in the hospital and at home, thus doctor gags would have wider appeal. Here are two gags about doctors, one an operation caption, the other Jewish:

> Don't worry about your operation . . . you're in
> competent hands . . .
> . . . all the nurses say your doctor is quite an
> operator!

(There is one quite limiting factor in the above card that most writers do not consider, and that is that the gag is a *pre*-operation gag, and most cards are sent *after* the operation. So watch your-self on this point. Make most of your operation gags *post-operation*.)

> It's easy to see that your doctor is kosher . . .
> . . . instead of penicillin he uses chicken soup!

Drinking: This theme often centers around the premise that drinking will make you well, or your illness may affect your drinking habits. It may also play on the idea of sneaking alcohol in to the patient:

> Thought I had a foolproof way of sneaking some
> of my homemade brew in to help you feel better . . .
> . . . but it ate a hole in your enema bag.

Missing You: This theme was a late entry into the *get well* category, but once it did come in it became highly popular, and it is obviously a logical theme to use for a *get well* card. Here's one:

> I've missed you so much since you've been in
> the hospital, I've become known as . . .
> . . . The Town Crier!

Joke: As in the other categories, a joke gag is always usable *if* it relates to the occasion in some manner. Here's a joke gag that shows how this theme can be used effectively in this category:

> To help you when you're ill, here's a simple
> way to take a bath in bed . . .
> . . . 1. Lock door. 2. Close all windows.
> 3. Fill room with $4\frac{1}{2}$ feet of warm water!

Topical: All the things said before about topical humor apply in here as well. Here is a topical gag that was used successfully during the mini-skirt craze:

> To help you get well, here is the latest, most
> up-to-date thing available . . .
> . . . a mini-bedpan! (small bedpan attachment)

Anniversary Themes

Complimentary: In the *anniversary* category, this theme may work a couple of ways. It may be used to compliment a couple on their marriage:

> You two have a marriage that would make even
> the President jealous . . .
>   . . . 'cause the *state of your union* is always great!

or it may be used for one spouse to compliment the other:

> Happy Anniversary from the one who makes the
> living . . .
>   . . . to the one who makes the living worthwhile!

Love: This theme is also used in different ways . . . one is to imply how the anniversary couple love and enjoy each other:

> You two are living proof that the couple
> who *play* together . . .
>   . . . stay together!

Another way is for one spouse to imply or state directly how much the other one is loved:

> Happy Anniversary to my ball and chain . . .
>   . . . from your prisoner of love!

Congratulations: This theme is used both to congratulate a couple on their wedding anniversary, and to congratulate someone celebrating an anniversary of any event — it could be buying a car, a new apartment or house, a business, or any of a dozen things. Obviously, gags are not written for each of these special events because they are too limited in nature. Instead, the gag is written as general as possible so that it can be sent for whatever type of anniversary may call for a congratulations card. Here's an example:

> Congratulations . . .
>   . . . looks like you've got a good thing going!

Joke: Everything said about the joke theme before applies here. Here's how one was used successfully in this category:

> Honey, you're doing so well as a wife . . .
> . . . I've decided to keep you for another year!

There you have them, a few of the themes used in the *everyday* categories, most of which can also be used in the *seasonal* categories. Naturally, there are many more themes and sub-themes than those few I have listed here. Those I have given you are not intended as the be-all and end-all of themes, but only as examples. Many of the themes from one category can readily be used in another category, even though I haven't shown all cases of this. In addition, as humor and sentiment change, new themes spring up while old ones die or become less popular. Of course, some of the new ones never become widely used, but they are often usable enough to garner a few sales for the alert free-lance writer.

Study the cards on the racks constantly for new themes and sub-themes. See how they're being used, write out some sort of specification for them as we have here, buy the cards or copy down the ideas in your ever-present notebook, and add the themes to your workroom list. It may be that a theme you pick up this way is perfect for you. It fits in with your background, likes, experiences, hobbies, and all the things that go to make up you and your humorous outlook on things. For example, some writers are whizzes at writing risque jokes; others, the cute, informal type of humor; and sentimentality simply flows from still others. So always be on the lookout for new themes that you can use . . . it's all money in your pocket. As a professional writer, you're in business for yourself, and no business can survive on old ideas and methods. Keep your business thriving with new, fresh ideas and themes.

Chapter XIII

Put Something on It

by H. Joseph Chadwick

Recently I had a visit from a talented greeting card writer whom we'll call Beverlee Brewer. Bev sells regularly to just about all the card companies, but she said she had a problem.

"You can't get anybody to help you carry your money to the bank." I said.

Bev forced herself not to laugh at my hilarity and said, "My problem is that for the life of me I can't write ideas using attachments, and it just destroys me because I know editors pay more money for them."

"Mucho more, usually," I said. "Mainly because editors get very few of them in the mail . . . probably less than 5 percent of the total number of ideas they receive. So attachment ideas are like at a premium."

"Well, if everybody else writes as many as I do, you're lucky if they get *any* in the mail."

"What's your big problem?" I asked.

"I guess my basic problem," Bev said, "is that I can't think of any attachments to use on greeting cards, and the few I do think of I don't know how to go about getting a gag for them. What comes first, the idea or the attachment?"

"In most cases the attachment. But there are times when the idea comes first, and it turns out to be the type of idea that can logically take an attachment, so you upgrade the card, make it more valuable, by putting an attachment on it. In most cases, and probably *all,* the attachment usually improves the idea itself."

"Okay," Bev said. "I believe you, but I don't know what you're talking about. So instead of trying to *tell* me about it, howsabout *showing* me how to write attachment ideas?"

"Well, since I'm a pushover for a girl of the opposite sex," I leered, "I'll show you all I know."

Bev edged slightly away from me. I ignored the obvious come-on and pulled open a file drawer marked ATTACHMENTS. The drawer contained several hundred cards that used attachments. "First on," I said, "let's take a look at some of the things that are being used as card attachments."

Bev joined me at the drawer and helped me to paw through the cards. Before long we had almost a hundred cards piled on my work table. While I read off the attachments on the cards, Bev listed them on a blackboard I sometimes use to diddle on. Some of the attachments were the actual, full-size items — for example, string and penny — while others were miniaturized versions, most of them made out of plastic. We separated the items into two lists. Here they are:

ACTUAL

Mirror	Confederate money	Straw
Calendar (small)	Zipper	Eraser
Stamp	Stone	Cork
Foreign money	Bell	Button
Checkers	Trading stamp	Corn pad
Candy	Bottle opener	Paperclip
Compass	Pepper pack	Whistle
Sandpaper	Play money	Comb (small to
Bag (paper and cloth)	Coil spring	oversized)
Beer bottle cap	Sucker (candy type)	Bathroom tissue
Salt pack	Copper wire	Cloth

Sugar pack	Swizzle stick	Balloon
Toothpick	Jelly bean	Bandaid
Rubber band	Alka-seltzer pack	String
Playing cards	Nail	Pin (Bobby,
Penny	Feather	straight, and
		safety)

MINIATURIZED

Screw	Bedpan	Hypodermic needle
Fan	Greeting card	Potty
Pill	Playing cards	Worm
Aspirin	Stethoscope	Mistletoe
Sun glasses	Ruby	Bowling ball
Crown	Star	Flower
Cocktail glass	Skeleton	Tooth
Gun	Tear drop	Bat (Flying and baseball)
Hanger	Broom	Leaf

After I called off the last item, Bev wrote it down and then stepped back and studied the board for a ding-ding and shook her head. "I never realized there were so many things that could be used as attachments."

"Well, even though the list is fairly long," I said, "I'm certain it's only a very small part of the number of things that *have* been, *can* be, and *will* be used on greeting cards. And, of course, the list contains nothing but *purchased* attachments, while many cards use *printed* attachments, and I'm sure there's no limit to the variety of printed attachments that can be used."

"Pardon my don't-know," Bev said, "but what's the difference between purchased attachments and printed attachments."

"Well, oddly enough, as the terms imply, purchased attachments are purchased; for example, bandaids, salt packs, mirrors, combs, and like so, while printed attachments are things that are die-cut and printed by the card publisher, like the miniature greeting cards that are sometimes used on the inside of a full-size card."

"I saw a graduation card the other day that had an attachment on the inside showing a character in a graduation cap and gown floating on a cloud marked Number 9. The attachment was held to the card by a small coil spring. I think the cover of the card said something like *Congratulations, Graduate!* and the inside said *How's the weather up there?* Now that was a printed attachment, wasn't it?"

"Right!" And there are many ideas that can be improved by using printed attachments like that, especially when the attachment is connected to the card by that coil spring you mentioned. It gives a jiggling action to the attachment when the card is opened. For example, recently I bought a Mother's Day card that said *I know a great mother when I see one! . . . and I see one RIGHT THERE!* Now the text by itself is just about a great big nothing, but the writer had put a character on the inside of the card with the character's right hand drawn slightly large and with the index finger pointing toward the person reading the card. Then the hand was cut out and put on a coil spring, so that it not only gave a three dimensional effect but it also wiggled as the card was opened. All in all, it was a very clever and effective attachment. And on top of that, it was simple and inexpensive to produce."

"It even sounds simple to think of," Bev said. "But I can never think of ideas like that."   ·

"That's probably because you're not really *thinking* attachments," I said, "especially the printed kind, which is a problem most free-lance writers seem to have. For example, I bought an idea that said on the cover *To a great guy on his birthday . . . Knowing how you like to keep in shape, I got you an exciting exercising apparatus . . .* The punchline on the inside of the card consisted solely of an illustration of a sexy girl. Now this as it was, was a cute semi-risque gag . . . but to help it along, I cut out the figure of the gal, put her on a coil spring, and attached her back to the inside of the card. Now when the card opened, the reader not only got a three dimensional effect from the attachment, but the wiggling and jiggling action from the coil spring tied in nicely with the sexy gal character and the *exercising* idea of the gag. Now, the point in all this is that I didn't do anything that the writer couldn't have done. And if she had, she would have earned herself almost half again what I paid her for the idea."

"Sounds like some of my ideas," Bev said. "Every time I see one of my finished gags that an editor has put an attachment on or made into a mechanical, I kick myself in the pagoda for not thinking of doing it myself!"

"Well, so that you won't end up with a sore pagoda," I said, "let's take our attachment list and write a few attachment gags."

"All right," Bev said, "but let me pick the attachment, something simple. How about a piece of string? That should make a good attachment, it's cheap and easy to get."

"Now that's using your beany," I said. "One of the first considerations a writer should give to an attachment is to see if it is inexpensive enough to use on a greeting card, and if it is readily available. Most card companies hold the cost of attachments down to about 5-percent of the retail price of the card, and this includes the hand labor involved in putting the attachment on the card. Yet some writers suggest attachments that are just far too costly and difficult to get. Just last week a writer suggested a half-burned wood match as an attachment. Now the gag was cute, but think of the time and labor involved in having girls burn matches half way down, and then try to attach them to cards without the burnt part falling off. Even if they could get a match on a card, imagine what would happen to the burnt part after the card had been handled a few times."

"It would bustacate," Bev said.

"Something like that," I said. "Yet writers keep suggesting things like that for attachments. Yesterday, a writer suggested a prune pit as an attachment. I could just see myself eating about 20,000 prunes to get the pits. I would not only get all wrinkled, but I would have other problems, too. So it's very important that you consider both the cost and the availability of the attachment you're suggesting. Neglecting either could ruin a sale."

"Okay," Bev said, "I'll remember both. Now how about the string?"

"Well, let's get a piece of string and take a look at it. I have some right here in my desk drawer. I like to handle the attachment I'm working on, take a look at it from different directions while I try to think of all the things you can do with it, or words that you can associate with it." I took a roll of string out of my drawer, cut off a short piece and held it up so Bev could see it. "Now here's the string, what can we do with it?"

Bev said, "We can tie it around our finger to remind us of something, like a birthday."

"Good! And how about tying a package up, or tying it between two things."

"Or we could tie one end to something and let the other end hang."

"You mean like the vines that Tarzan swings on?"

"Yes," Bev said.

"What else could we tie it to?" I asked.

"Well, besides our finger, I suppose we could tie it to other places on ourselves. Our wrists, arm, leg, toes, ankles, neck, hands . . ." She stopped and giggled.

"What's funny?" I asked.

"When I thought of hands," Bev said, "I could picture myself holding one end of the string in each hand and trying to jump rope with it, sort of the *world's smallest jump-rope*. Or maybe a *mini jump-rope*. But that's kind of silly!"

"Good! When trying to think of what to do with an attachment, *be* silly! *Be* wild! *Be* ridiculous! Don't hold your imagination back, let it run free, bounce it off the walls, the floor, the ceiling, the sky. Don't stiffle it by trying to keep it within some imaginary bounds. Let it think of all the cockeyed, silly, wild, ridiculous, nonsensical things you can do with an attachment. Look at the attachment backwards, sideways, upside-down, inside-out, frontside-back, backside-front. That's the only way your imagination can come up with really funny stuff!"

"Okay," Bev said. She took the string from me and dangled it in front of her. "Imagination go crazy!" Then she made a face. "Nothing's happening."

"Then do something with the string, don't let it be static."

She tied it around her finger. Too tightly, and her finger started to turn blue. She made another face. "If I left this on my finger too long I'd get gangrene and my finger would fall off." This time her face made a grin. "Hey! How about if we use that first thing we said we could do with a string . . . tie it around our finger to remember a birthday . . . and we keep it on all year long and our . . ." She stopped for a think, and then commanded as all women writers do: "Write this down, Sir!" I applied my paper to the pencil and she said, "We attach a piece of string to the cover of the card, and then we say, *Last year I tied this string around my finger so I would remember your birthday . . . today my finger fell off! Happy Birthday!*"

"By golly," I said, "I think you've got it!"

"And if I went to a hospital," Bev said, "I bet I could get

rid of it." Then she grinned again. "You know, instead of tying this string to our finger, we could tie it to our leg so we wouldn't fall out of a hospital bed."

"Not bad," I said. "But not particularly funny. Why not tie it to your big toe? The big toe is funnier than the leg."

"And the belly button is funnier than the stomach, and the fanny is funnier than the back," Bev said. "But even with the string tied to the big toe, the idea still isn't funny enough, is it?"

"No, because there really isn't anything funny about falling out of bed. It's not like falling off your bedpan."

Bev hit me. "Or *into* your bedpan!" she almost screamed. She commanded me again: "Write this down, Knave!" I wrote.

"We put a piece of string on the cover," she said, "then we say, *To keep you from worrying while you're ill, here's the latest sickroom aid. Tie one end of string to your big toe. Tie other end of string to the bedpost . . . There! Now you won't fall into your bedpan!*"

"Okay, smart gal," I said. "Now it's my turn. We said that one thing we could do with the string was tie one end to something and let the other end hang like the vines Tarzan swings on . . . right?!"

"Right!"

"Okay," I said. "Now *you* write this down. On the cover of the card, we say, *For your birthday here's a little something to help you have a real swinging time . . .* Inside the card we tape a piece of string, mark one end *A* and the other end *B*, then we say, *1. Tie end A to limb of tree. 2. Hold end B in both hands. 3. Now have a swinging birthday!!!*"

"Not bad for a beginner," Bev said.

I bowed. "We humble folks thank the Great Ones for any and all kind words."

Bev ignored my fantastic humor and studied our list of attachments. "Let's try another attachment," she said. "How about a worm?"

I hunted through my box of attachments until I found a small plastic worm in a zigzag shape. I handed it to Bev. "One worm at your peck and call."

Again she displayed masterly control by not going into helpless hysterics over my repartee. "Do we do the same thing with this that we did with the string?" she asked. "Think of all the things we can that a worm does or is or what you can do with it or whathaveyou?"

"That's the best way to start."

"Well, first of all you can fish with a worm," Bev said.

"When I was a kid," I said, "I used to like to fish with my dad."

Bev ignored me again. I was beginning to have doubts about her sense of humor. "And you can dig them out of the ground and sell them."

"And you can put one in a jar and keep it for a pet," I said. "Just in case your mother won't let you have a dog."

Bev gave me a strange look that made me wonder about her, and then said, "And worms crawl on the ground and live under rocks."

"They also crawl *in* the ground," I said, "and live in old logs and dead trees."

Bev nodded thoughtfully. "You know I was just thinking, isn't there a fairly common expression about *left no stone unturned?*"

"Yes," I said. "It means you looked everywhere possible for something or other."

"Well, since worms are often found under rocks," Bev said "and you fish with them, I bet we could combine those two things with the expression and make a fisherman's birthday card."

"Like how?"

"Like we could say on the cover, *Left no stone unturned to find the perfect birthday gift for a great fisherman like you!* On the inside of the card we could have just the *worm attachment,* and the tag line *Happy Birthday.*"

"Now I *know* you've got it!" I said.

"All right, Bev said, "how about you giving a go?!"

"Okay, let's take the thought of worms living in old logs and combine it, as you just did, with an old expression, in this case, *aged in wood,* which of course refers to a process used for good booze!"

"Leave it to you to bring booze into the act," Bev said.

I ignored her. "Then we can write a gag that says on the card cover something like, *For your birthday here's a little something that's been aged in wood for over twenty years!* On the inside of the card we'll attach the worm, and say, *The world's oldest worm!!! Happy Birthday!*

"Not bad," Bev said. "Keep it up and I'll make a writer out of you yet."

"Thanks, luv," I said. "Would you like to try one last one?"

"Okay," Bev said. She ran down the attachment list. "How about a salt pack?" she said.

I rummaged through my attachment box and found a small package of salt, like the ones you get at carry-out restaurants. I held it up so Bev could see it. "Here tis. Now what is salt good for, what can you do with it, what does it do?"

"Well, it's a seasoning for food, some people put it in beer, it's used on salted nuts . . ."

"And it makes you thirsty if you eat too much of it," I said.

"And in the winter it's used to break up, or melt, I guess, ice," Bev said.

"That's right. And how about sprinkling salt on a bird's tail."

"Hey! That *sprinkling* thing you just said gave me an idea," Bev said.

"It's about time you admitted that I give you ideas," I told her.

Her control was magnificent as she said, "We can tie it in with the *salted nuts* thing."

"How so?" I asked.

"Well, a person who's *nicely crazy* is sometimes called a *nut* . . . right?"

"Right!"

"Okay . . . then howsabout if we say something like, *Here's a magic gift for your birthday! Just sprinkle the contents of the enclosed package over your head and you will be instantly adored!!! . . .* Inside we put the salt pack, and say, *by people who love salted nuts!!!*"

I flipped my hand, "For a beginner, s'all right."

"Okay, Hot One," Bev sneered, "let's see you come up with one."

"R-R-RIGH-T-T!" I said, doing my great imitation of Bill Cosby. "Let's use the one about putting salt into beer. We could put the salt pack inside the card and cut a hole through the cover of the card just large enough so the pack would show . . ."

Bev interrupted me. "Why not just put the pack on the cover?"

"Because after a card customer looks at a card in a store, he usually puts it back into the rack pocket by sliding it down the front of one of the cards already in the pocket, watch how you do this yourself next time you're in a store looking at cards. Anywho, if the cards already in the pocket have attachments on the cover, the card sliding down across their front will usually catch on the attachments and either knock them off or damage them. So card companies tend not to put attachments on the covers of cards. If an attachment has to show on the front of the card because of the gag, the peephole design I just mentioned, is usually used. There are exceptions to this, of course, but it's usually when the art director wants a different look on the front of the card and is willing to take the chance of having the attachment damaged, even though the sales manager may not be too crazy about it. Sokay?"

"Sokay!" Bev said.

"Anyhey," I said, "We now have the salt inside the card with a hole cut in the card cover so the pack will show through. We then say *If I were you, I'd take all this birthday hullabaloo with a grain of salt . . . dropped into a stein of beer!*"

"Very good!" Bev said. "Especially for a rank . . ."

"Thank you again, luv," I said. "Now for a last one before we close that Great Door In The Mind, how about something like this, *Here's a little birthday gift for someone who only drinks when thirsty . . .* Inside we put a salt pack and the tag line *Happy Birthday.* How's that sound?"

"Like it came from the soul of a poet," Bev said. "And now, before we fade into the sunset, where do I get attachments from? Or to put it another way, from where do I get attachments?"

"A lot of the attachments you can get in variety-type department stores, five and tens. Things like blotters, sponges, paper clips, bottle openers, bags, and like so. Something I often do is just browse through the store looking for anything inexpensive enough and small enough to be used on a card. And speaking of small, the size of your attachment is one very important thing to take into consideration. Don't suggest anything heavy (eats up postage), sharp (cuts the card), bulky (takes up too much room in the box when the cards are shipped to the dealer, and too much room in the racks), or overly long or wide (must fit inside area of card). Lots of good attachment gags are rejected for just one of those four reasons."

"Okay, I'll watch," said Bev. "Now besides department stores, where else can I find attachments?"

"Well, try some of the *small* variety stores that sell knick-knacks, tricks, and games, or some of the catalog gift houses like Spencer and Hanover House. Buy a couple of things from them so you can get on their mailing lists and receive their new catalogs. You can sometimes run into a gold mine."

Of course, one of the most logical places to get attachments is from greeting cards themselves, especially the kind of attachments you can't find in normal retail outlets. For the price of the greeting card, you can get an attachment that coupled with a good gag could give you a sale worth a hundred times what you paid for the card. So it's a pretty good investment."

"I'll invest," Bev said, then added, "I guess if you're going to write attachment ideas, you must be constantly on the lookout for anything and everything, anywhere and everywhere, that could be used as an attachment."

"You couldn't be more right," I said. "Actually, it's nothing more than an attitude, a frame of mind, a way of looking at everything as it relates to greeting cards. And if you want to make money in this business, that's got to be your bag."

"Speaking of bags," Bev said, "I've got to skit. You're a lover for taking all this time to explain attachments to me. I'll buy you the biggest drink in town with the first check I get for an attachment idea."

"You've got a ding-ding," I said.

As Bev swayed out the door, she looked back over her shoulder and grinned at me sideways.

And I don't know why.

Chapter XIV

Make It Move

by H. Joseph Chadwick

In this chapter we are going to discuss the type of cards that most, and perhaps all, greeting card writers consider the hardest to do; and those are cards in which something moves, some action takes place when the card is opened. This type of card is commonly called a *mechanical.*

Although most writers consider mechanicals difficult to do, I have a feeling that the difficulty comes from a lack of study and devoting enough creative time and thinking to them. It's not hard to understand why writers give less time and thought to them. After all it's easier to write a greeting card gag than it is to try to work out *new* mechanics for getting paper and metal and things to fold and open and move in the right direction. And though the money is better for mechanicals, it takes more time to put a mechanical dummy together and try to make it work than it does to write a simple non-mechanical gag. So what's the sense in a writer trying to make *new* mechanical cards?

No sense! Not in trying to make *new* mechanical cards anyway! Besides, most large companies have designers whose full time job is to come up with new and original mechanicals, and you can't hope to compete with these trained and experienced people on new designs. But you can compete with them on *ideas* by adapting and modifying the action of mechanical cards already on the racks to give you a slightly different action with a new gag, or simply writing a new gag for the action as it is.

After you've done that, send the idea to the editor whose company published the card, telling him that you've adapted one of his mechanicals to a new gag, or have written a new gag to the mechanical as it is, and you think he might be interested in it. If he isn't, and returns the idea to you without comment, then send it on to another editor who buys mechanicals, telling him what you've done in adapting the action or writing a new gag for it. They know you aren't suggesting they use exactly the same presentation and art work, but only the basic action and your new gag. If you don't think they will know it, tell them. And don't worry about the legality of it. It's all perfectly legal and ethical. You cannot copyright an idea, only its presentation, so a new gag, new art work, new layout, different dimensions, and everything else that goes into a redesign of a mechanical card add up to a completely new and different presentation — and all legal and ethical.

Would any editor *resent* your sending him an adaption or a new gag for a mechanical card published by his or some other company? I wouldn't, and several other editors I've talked to wouldn't either. And I think any editor who would, would have to be a little narrow minded and doing a poor job as editor. Why? Because he knows as well as we do that greeting card companies are continually using *versions* of mechanicals developed by other companies, or just writing new gags for the action and using it basically as it is, with their own art work and presentation, of course. It's part and parcel of the game. And it's no secret within the industry that it's done, or that it's expected to be done. It's silly to let a good mechanical sit around static when there may be dozens of ideas that could be written for it. And there is no difference in different companies using basically the same mechanical than there is in their using the same attachments.

As editor of Barker Greeting Cards, the largest publisher of mechanical cards, I saw dozens of *adaptions* of our mechanicals being used by other companies. And my only feeling when I saw them was self-recrimination because I hadn't thought of the different gag for the mechanical myself, mixed, of course, with a little envy and admiration for whoever wrote the gag.

So buy some of the mechanicals on the market that you feel you could adapt and write new gags for, and give them a try with the editor whose company put the idea out. If he doesn't like the idea of your using one of their cards that way, he'll tell you, foolishly, of course, but maybe that's his bag. (Just for the record, there are no foolish editors right at the moment, but you never know what might show up in the future! Keep your eyes open and let me know if you spot any.)

Now let's take a look at a few mechanicals and see how new gags can be written for them, and how some of them can be modified slightly to make basically new actions, and anything else we can think to do with them. Once we've become familiar with some of the basic actions that can be performed by cards, we'll also take a look at some of the regular gags you write and put an action to them. There's a very simple principle to follow when doing this. But first we'll look at writing different gags for the same mechanical, one already published.

Barker Greeting Cards has a mechanical that has been in their line for years (and has showed up in everyone else's line, too), and that is consistently their #1 selling mechanical card. The action in the card duplicates the way a child will sometimes exuberantly throw his arms out wide apart to express an idea or add emphasis to his words, sort of like the way a fisherman shows how big the one was that got away. Figure 1A shows how the card looks when it's closed; in Figure 1B the card is shown open.

FIG. 1A   FIG. 1B

The character on the cover of the card, and the face inside, are shown happy because the card expresses love: *Wanna know how much I love you? . . . THIS MUCH!* This same expression and open arms action would also fit these gags:

> Wanna know how much I wish you a Happy Birthday? . . .
> . . . THIS MUCH!
> THANKS . . .
> . . . SO MUCH!
> If you want your Christmas present from me . . .
> . . . come and get it!

Now let's put a sad, perhaps even tearful, face on the inside, as shown in Figure 2B.

Besides the text on the card, *Wanna know how much I miss you? . . . THIS MUCH,* the sad expressions and open arms action

FIG. 2A   FIG. 2B

would fit both of these gags:

> FORGIVE ME . . .
> . . . PLEASE!
> Wanna know how much I'm sorry you're sick? . . .
> . . . THIS MUCH!

Beginning to get the idea? Sure you are! And now you probably want to know how you go about writing ideas like this for an action you already have?

My method is the simplest and most direct there is . . . I sit and play with the card, opening and closing it, watching the action, seeing how it works, what it does, what emotion or natural human action it might express. Sometimes I turn the card upside down or sideways, both of which give you a different viewpoint and perspective on the action. In the case of the arms card, for which I wrote all the gags except the original *Wanna know how much I love you?* and *Wanna know how much I miss you?,* I always tried to think of all the emotions people express by throwing their arms apart, emotions that could be tied into a greeting card occasion. And though I came up with quite a few, I'm sure there are still dozens more that can be written around that one action.

Here's another mechanical card that we wrote numerous gags for, and that I'm certain has room for many more gags.

FIG. 3A   FIG. 3B

As shown in Figures 3A and 3B, the mechanical consists of a sliding panel that passes between an acetate window and the inside background of the card. Both the acetate window and the background have something drawn on them. When the card is closed, the drawing on the acetate shows through the hole in the card cover, but the background drawing is hidden by the sliding panel. When the card is opened, the panel slides over and the drawing on the background now becomes part of the drawing on the acetate . . . they are mixed together. This is a very simple mechanical to make, even if you start from scratch and make your own dummy.

This brings up the point that if you wish to submit your own dummy rather than a published mechanical, or if you want to change the original mechanical somehow, you can very easily make a dummy by carefully taking apart the published mechanical card, laying all the pieces out on the paper stock you are going to use. (Make certain your stock is heavy enough, yet not too heavy. Best bet is to try to match the weight of the paper in the published card.), trace out the pieces, and then cut them out. The final step, of course, is to put the pieces together as they were in the published card. Be certain to examine the published card carefully before you take it apart, and perhaps even mark it some way, or you may forget how it went together. Another point: some of your illustrations, colors, etc., may have to go on before you glue your dummy together. Be sure to check for this.

Now here's another card that uses the same acetate mechanical as the one in Figures 3A and 3B.

FIG. 4A   FIG. 4B

And here are some more gags we wrote using the above mechanical:

> (A woman in a plain dress and apron was shown on the acetate . . . the cover text said:) Here it is Mother's Day and you're wearing the same thing you do every day . . .
> . . . (When the card was opened, a golden halo and wings appeared over and on the woman.)
> (A simple character, full view, was shown on the acetate . . . the text read:) Congratulations, Graduate . . .
> . . . (When the card was opened, the character appeared to be dressed in a graduation cap and gown .. . the text said:) . . . your dream has come true!

Those are only a couple of the several cards we did using that particular mechanical, but there are many many more still to be done, probably by you. Want to think of some quick-like, right now? Let's try it.

How about using that old gag *Without you . . . I get blue!?* I bet you already see how it would work, don't you? We would put a simple character on the acetate, then color the background under the acetate blue. So when the card was opened, the character would actually turn blue to go along with the expression *I get blue.* (And maybe about here you might start getting a glimpse of how you can make mechanicals out of some of your regular gags, those that play around a word or expression that denotes an action or a change. Think about it while we try some more gags with our acetate mechanical.)

We could write a couple more *Without you* gags that would go alone with this mechanical. For example, how about *Without you . . . it's hell! . . .?* We could put a simple character on the acetate, and then draw flames and rocks and maybe a sign saying *HELL* on the background. Then when the card was opened, the character would now appear to be *in hell.*

And how about *Without you . . . I'm shot! . . .?* We could use a simple character on the acetate again, but this time punch the background, the card itself, full of holes. Now when the card is opened, the character will appear to be *shot* full of holes.

Now try some gags of your own around this mechanical. Several companies use it, or some version of it, and I'm sure they would consider any new gags *you* could come up with. (The two *we* just came up with I'm claiming as my own. Sorry, bubie!)

Let's take a quick look at a couple more mechanicals and then talk about tying mechanicals to gags you've already written. The principle behind the mechanical shown in Figures 5A and 5B is that something — in this case, a mail box — opens when you open the card. Now, this *something* could be a box, a door, an oven, or anything that you can think of that *opens.* Try some gags around that principle once in a while.

FIG. 5A   FIG. 5B

Figures 6A and 6B show an action that is very similar to the arms action that we have already talked about, but here the full figure is used. Notice that we could use with this action one of the same gags we used with the arms card: and this is, *If you want your Christmas (or Birthday or Valentine's Day) present from me . . . come and get it!* We could also use a gag with this card that said something like: *For your birthday I wanted to send you something simple but fun . . . so here I am, simple but fun!*

FIG. 6A   FIG. 6B

Now let's see if you've got any ideas that we could make into mechanical cards. They can, remember, usually be done with any gag that denotes a change or an action of some kind. Figures 7A and 7B show a mechanical that was developed from a good selling 25¢ *non-mechanical* card. The cover of this card, which isn't shown, says (based on a cigarette commercial): *Valentine, you're absolutely the GREATEST, the most SATISFYING, the least IRRITATING, the COOLEST, in fact . . .* Figure 7A shows the inside of the card with the action half completed. In Figure 7B, the action is fully completed.

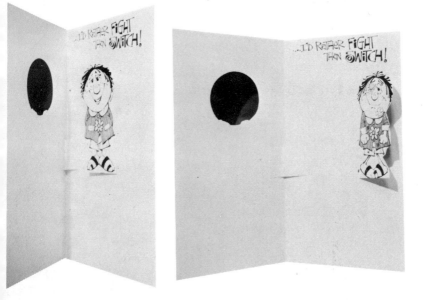

FIG. 7A   FIG. 7B

As you can see from the illustrations, the character has been *switched* — to show he actually has been fighting. And I'm certain that you're thinking at this moment, or were just going to, that since this *switch* denotes a change, this same gag could be used with our acetate mechanical. The character would be shown normal on the acetate, and then shown with black eyes and bandages when the card is opened. Good thinking!

Let's suppose now that you wrote a card that said something like *Valentine, you've been giving me a lot of lip lately . . .* (and inside you drew a picture of a pair of lips . . . and said:) *and I want more!* This could be turned into a mechanical by using the action on the card shown in Figures 8A and 8B. As you can see, when this card is opened, the head comes out toward the reader. Almost the same design could be used for your gag, the one you've just written.

FIG. 8A   FIG. 8B

And how about if you came up with a timely gag that said something like *Thought you might like one of those snappy little MUSTANGS for your birthday . . .* (and on the inside you attach a small plastic horse . . . and the text inside said:) *. . . here's one with lots of kick!* Now since *kick* denotes an *action* we should be able to make a mechanical out of it, maybe one that would show a mustang kicking up his heels. Like the one shown in Figure 9. This is a double-action mechanical in the sense that both the top and the bottom of the figure move. Watch for this kind because they're great. A lot of action takes place when the card is opened, that's the kind of card most editors who do mechanicals like to get hold of.

FIG. 9

While we're on the subject of multiple-action cards, it's a good place to bring up the point that one effective method of coming up with fairly fresh mechanical ideas is to change the number of actions on a card. If the original mechanical has a double-action, can you remove one of the actions and come up with something different? Can you combine a couple of single actions from different cards? Can you add an action to a double-action and come up with an effective triple-action? How about combining an action with an attachment, especially one that will make a noise, like a bell?

Now that you have sight (reading the card), movement (the action), and sound (the bell ringing) combined on one card, can you add any other sensations? Feel and odor? Could you combine them all on one card? Fresh combinations? Think about it.

Also think about maintaining the same basic action on a card, but changing the figures. For example, could the mustang on the card we just discussed be a man driving? Or with small additions, someone dancing? Could the arms on our "Wanna know how much . . ." card be *wings* . . . or a *sleigh* and *reindeers?* Turn the action, twist it, look at it every possible way you can.

You see, writing mechanicals, even from scratch, isn't so hard after all, is it? And it's a nice break from the routine of writing regular non-moving gags, not to mention the fact that the money's better. So the next time you're down at the corner drug store, the pool hall, that strange house on the other street, or wherever your favorite greeting card racks are, spend a few bucks on some good mechanicals. Then take them home, look them over, figure out how they work, play with them, get used to them. And keep them within reach of your work area so you can handle and think about them frequently. Before you know it, you'll be thinking mechanicals with every card you write.

While you're down at your favorite place looking at mechanicals, study the way people handle them, the way they put them back into the racks, how many times the same card is handled, and how roughly.

One problem that many new writers have when they develop mechanical cards is that they think only of the card being opened that first time when the receiver gets it. They don't consider the many times the card may be opened by potential buyers in the store, or that the receiver may look at the card several times, or show it to friends numerous times. So they develop mechanicals that are either self-destructing when the card is opened, or that are so delicate the card couldn't be opened more than two or three times without destroying the action. Watch these points.

Also watch that you don't design a mechanical that doesn't *reset itself* when the card is closed. For example, a large paper flower might unfold when the card is opened, but the card is designed so that the flower has to be refolded by the person opening the card. You can count on about one out of every twenty customers to refold such a thing . . . most of them will simply shove the card back into the rack. You can imagine what would happen to this card in short order, to say nothing of the store owner's patience.

If you become familiar with the various types of rack damage that can happen to a mechanical card, you will know what designs to avoid. Check cards that are already damaged and try to figure out why they got damaged. Perhaps the damage could have been prevented by a better design. Talk to the store owner or clerks about the whys and wherefores of damaged cards. These people are fountains of information, and can often pinpoint design problems. Check anything, everything, and everyone for information that might affect your development of a mechanical idea. Remember, when an editor looks at your mechanical, he's looking at it as a finished card sitting in a rack waiting for somebody to buy it. To sell him, you have to look at it that way too!

One final point. Unlike attachment ideas where you can simply suggest the attachment if you don't have one, with mechanical ideas you must send the editor a working mechanical card. He cannot properly evaluate your idea otherwise, and he certainly isn't going to *make* a mechanical for you to see whether or not your idea will work. That's your job. Do it! (One writer recently suggested a complicated mechanical to me, and then at the end of his letter said, "If after you make the card up you decide you don't want to buy it, would you please send the made-up card to me so I can submit it to someone else.")

There are very *rare* exceptions to the rule of sending the editor a working dummy, but they are so rare I'm not even going to go into them. *This* is the only rule you should work by: *If you want to sell the editor a mechanical idea, send him a working mechanical dummy,* whether it's one you made from scratch yourself, an adaption of a published card, or the published card as it is. If you're not willing to take the time and effort to do this, forget about mechanical ideas. You're just wasting the editor's time — and your own.

Lastly, remember the basic principle to the whole thing: *a mechanical card can usually be made from any idea that denotes by word, expression, or even implication, some form of action or change.* Are there exceptions to this? Of course! There are exceptions to everything, except death. And you'll see the exceptions on the racks without my having to give you examples here. But for writing gags for mechanicals on an occasional basis, you'll find that it will be a lot easier and you'll spend less time and waste less if you stick to the basic principle I've given you.

In case you're wondering whose principle it is, it's mine. But it works for me, so why not for you?

Chapter XV

Mottos, Buttons, and Humorous Stationery

by George F. Stanley, Jr.

Three of the fastest selling impulse items in the humorous field today are mottos, buttons, and stationery. Young people, from their teens to mid-twenties, are the principal buyers of these items. They buy mottos to tack to their walls, tuck into their mirrors, put on their desks, and to send to each other. They buy buttons to wear as personal little protests or as a shock factor or just to be different. They buy stationery to write to each other, and sometimes even to older straight-laced people. They like it both because it's different and because of the humor and bright modern colors in it.

All three of these items use the same basic near-protest, philosophical, "I don't give a damn! if you're shocked, baby, that's good!" type of humor. Once in awhile sentimentality creeps in, but not very often. Why are these items so popular with the young people? Lots of question marks. Maybe it's their way of saying "If we don't laugh and make fun of the way things are in this world, the way people act, and the shape everything is in, then, baby, we're gonna cry!"

Whatever their reasons, a look at some of the things they're buying will give you a few hints on where to get ideas and how to write them.

Mottos: The dictionary defines a *motto* as "a phrase, or word, expressive of one's guiding principle," but the word has been so broadened in the humorous market that this particular definition doesn't apply except in isolated instances. If you were looking for a definition that would fit humorous mottos, it might be that they are "twisted philosophies." In fact, as you go through our examples of good selling mottos and buttons, you'll find that many of them are humorous twists on old straight mottos, slogans, philosophies, and just plain sayings. For example, the straight motto "If at first you don't succeed, try, try, again!" has now been twisted into this humorous motto: "If at first you don't succeed . . . blame somebody." And the slogan "Avoid hangovers, don't drink" has now become "Avoid hangovers . . . stay drunk!"

When you're looking for ideas and sources of material, check some of the old expressions, quotations, clichés, slogans; especially those collections of these items that are so plentiful today, such as those by Esar and Harral, and of course the old standby *Bartlett's Familiar Quotations.*

Here are some examples that demonstrate the wide range of humor in mottos:

Drinking: I never drink more than three times a day . . .
. . . morning, noon, and night!

Sex: The shortest speech I ever heard on the subject of sex . . . it gives me great pleasure . . .

Egotism: I'm not a bit conceited . . . that's one of the reasons why I'm so great!

Work Situations: This job is so confusing, I occasionally do something right.

Married Life: Notice! . . . I am the boss in this house . . . and I've got my wife's permission to say so!

Within these popular subjects, general types of written copy would include the following. I believe there is more copy for

umorous mottos using the word "I" than any other word. For
example:

	I always dreamed of a rosy future and sure enough, here I am in the red.
Using "We":	We have fast workers, and we have slow workers, but most of our workers are half fast workers.
Conditions:	Around here a man advances as far as his secretary let's him!
Notices:	Gone for coffee . . . back in time for lunch;
Creeds:	If positive thinking fails . . . try positive drinking!
Play on Words:	This place is full of willing people, some willing to work and the rest willing to let them!

Notice the large number of categories you can funnel your
ideas for mottos into.

Some mottos to be completely effective must be accompanied
by an appropriate illustration. This is especially true in a category that I refer to as *sophisticated or low key mottos.* The copy
doesn't necessarily have to be completely humorous. Here are
several examples of what I mean. One illustration has a neuter
character looking out of an outhouse with a caption *"I'm so
confused . . . this is the only place I'm sure of what I'm doing,"*
or, a character lying down surrounded by empty cans of booze with
caption *"I'm definitely going to shape up right after this week-
end,"* or, an illustration of a couple mournfully looking at each
other exclaiming *"I know we'll never stop being happy . . . once
we get started."*

Be sure to keep your copy as short as possible. Most mottos
have only one or two words such as *I'm broad-minded,* or *Nobody
loves me.* Most buyers of mottos are not going to take the time
to read long copy, so shorter copy sells better.

One of the classic mottos should be mentioned. Probably

the best seller of all depicts a character with a banner containing the word *sex.* It says:

I'm no authority, but I know what I like!

Buttons: Imagine a typical campaign button, full of color, bu instead of the name of a candidate, for example, there would be short humorous copy. These are the types of buttons that we are talking about. The size varies from one inch in diameter up to three inches in diameter, but the most popular is one and three-quarters inches in diameter. For this reason, it is extremel important to keep your copy as short as possible. Too man words would make it hard to read. Copy for buttons has to hav an instantaneous punch line to get the desired attention.

Young people buy most buttons and represent the principa market. However, for social gatherings, it is not unusual to se middle-aged button users. Quite naturally the purchase of but tons (and they are often bought as a multiple sale) is as a impulse item. The motivation behind many sales results fror a personal connection that refers to a circumstance or event i the buyer's life.

There is a wide range of humor and the many categories men tioned for mottos could also apply to buttons. Certainly th

Egotism category applies to buttons with such mottos as,

Handle me! I'm a living doll!

Don't stare . . . I know I'm good looking!

There is a greater tendency these days to write much mor risque button copy. Certainly the copy of the protest buttor are some examples. There are many button suppliers that thriv on downright filth, and let's face it, a large segment of th public purchases this type of copy.

Risque copy, but using the double meaning to a small degre characterizes another type button. For example:

Undercovers Agent!

If it feels good, I'll do it!

There are also buttons that read:

My button loves your button!

Warning! I am naked underneath my clothes.

Humorous Stationery: The type of humorous stationery most popular now on the market is a tablet (or boxed sheets with envelopes) with twenty-four pages including two each of twelve different designs, with accompanying copy written around a single theme.

The best way to present your copy to an editor is to select a theme, then a clever title, and finally copy for at least twelve different pages. Several alternate pages is advisable in the event the editor might be interested in the theme ideas as a unit but may not approve all twelve copy ideas sent in.

The subject matter can be broad, from copy based on the general theme of *Missing you,* to a definite or specific theme, such as, *voting, fashions, animals,* etc.

Most of the copy is humorous, but it doesn't necessarily have to be, and one tablet in our line is sentimental, almost mushy, but it is selling very well. As an example of this, we entitled this humorous assorted tablet, *Passionate Notes for Someone Dear,* as a semi-provocative lead in. It is based on probably the most popular overall subject matter, which is the *missing you* theme. Girls purchase most of this material primarily because they are more sentimental by nature, and because more boys are away from home attending college or in service. Thus, it is advisable to write most copy in the *missing you* category from the feminine viewpoint.

Many of the sheets in a set begin with a similar phrase. For example, notice the copy from two of the pages in the *Passionate Notes* tablet.

Consider yourself thought about . . . Oooh! What I'm thinking.

Consider yourself felt about . . . love that feeling.

The most popular tablet in the Vagabond line is entitled *Dear John*. Most editors are aware that such subjects as sex and bathroom humor sell extremely well. Of course, we try to keep the humor in good taste. Some examples of the inside pages from *Dear John* with appropriate illustrations are:

This note is a Go-Go.

Thought I'd get right to the seat of the matter.

Much of the original subject matter for assorted stationery revolves around the general statements of *I'll Write Soon,* or *I Would Have Written Sooner.* As an example, a typical page may have combined such printed copy as *Please Write Soon* illustrated with a sad looking girl leaning against a mailbox surrounded by cobwebs.

After the popular acceptance of this type of humorous stationery, take-offs in all directions followed. Many buyers of stationery have apparently found it more interesting to send a note with a humorous dialogue and illustration than a piece of blank paper. Now we have discovered that themes based on funny captains with no basic relationship to a piece of writing paper have as much popularity as any other theme. In our line we have humorous captions based on *foot-prints,* which we call *Foot Notes,* and another tablet entitled *Shape Up,* in which there are clever captions based on *squares* and *triangular shaped blocks.*

Some titles in our line which would have a general theme are *P.S.; Noteable Notes,* or *Let It Out.* The illustrations and copy are such that they could apply to both men and women of all ages for all purposes. We always favor general themes for selling purposes because they apply to a larger segment of the population. Now and then, however, we do ask our writers to contribute specific themes. Here is some of the copy from *travel* theme. At the top of each page is a special line reading, *Hello from . . .* or, *Greetings from . . .* then the copy is written at the bottom. For example:

People are so friendly here . . .
The minute we arrived they held out their hands to us . . . palms up!

Or beside an illustrated picnic table with a bear in the background, the copy reads:

There's nothing like a beautiful park, open air, etc., to make
you hungry as a BEAR!

Or beside a giant waterfall, the copy reads:

Gee, I hope I remembered to turn off the shower!

There are very few limitations on writing copy for humorous stationery. The subject material can range from a central theme (circus, devils, cats, outhouses, etc.) to unusual captions similar to those in a cartoon book, or to the basic general theme of *I Miss You,* or *I'll Be Writing Soon.* For example:

HISTORICAL HYSTERIA (humorous notes written by famous
people in history such as Napoleon,
Benjamin Franklin, Samson, etc.)

MOD MAD PAD (spoofing the latest fashions)

Try to submit an appropriate, catchy title for the overall tablet. It is also wise to signify on your copy a helpful guide to the illustrator in creating the accompanying art work.

The range of opportunities in writing copy for the stationery market has been broadened by the new found popularity of mottos, buttons, and humorous stationery. Each of these items is somewhat different, but the basic ingredient found in all of them is clever humor with good *"catch-phrases"* that arouse the interest of the impulse stationery buyer. When you write, remember these points: Write short, snappy, catchy ideas for impulse buyers who are somewhere between 13 and 25 years old.

It's that simple, which isn't of course, *that* simple.

Chapter XVI

How To Get Funny Ideas When You're Alone

by Jack E. Schneider

This, as the title hints, is a chapter on how to get funny ideas when you're alone. Why the *alone* is beyond me. When the editor laid this chapter on me to do, the title came with it. Personally, I wanted to do a chapter on how to get funny ideas while lying on a tiger-skin rug in front of a roaring fireplace reading the latest unexpurgated edition of *Alice In Wonderland* to a warm female. But since I lacked the experience of having done so, and the editor would not advance me any research funds to do so, I came back down to earth, took a cold shower, and accepted the bitter *without* the sweet. It would have made a heckuva chapter though . . . I could almost see the bids for the movie rights rolling in, see the title flashing on the marquees: *"Alice In Wonderland Revisited* or *How to Get Funny Ideas While Lying On A Tiger-Skin Rug In Front Of A Roaring Fireplace Reading . . ."* BUT, I had to accept the inevitable . . . nothing worthwhile ever comes of casting swine before pearls . . . or ruths, or marys.

So in this chapter we will deal with the various methods used to get funny ideas, better known as how to write humor. We will explain the methods of generating humor, namely: association, characteristics, and switching. We'll also explain and demonstrate how to use the various humor formulas — exaggeration, insult, reverse, clichés, combinations, definition, misunderstanding, literal (truth), play-on-words, repetition, whimsy, topical, and zany.

Those are the tools of the trade in the humor or gag writing profession. Let me draw a parallel to point up what I mean by tools. Let's say you decide to change the shade of your office walls from bourbon blue to wino red. You go out and pick up a few cans of wino red, a brush, roller and tray, etc. Now you lug all this paraphernalia to your office, and you sit down . . . and wait . . . and nothing happens. I suppose by this time you're already ahead of me. And you're right!

The walls don't get painted until you take the tools and put them to use. The same thing applies to humor. We can give you the tools to work with, the methods and formulas for generating humor, but from there on it's you and your sense of humor that have got to do the work. The *funny business* is WORKING at the business of being funny!

Humor method: *Association.*

Let's assume that you want to write a studio birthday card. On a sheet of paper, list all the words you can think of that are *associated* with birthdays. For example:

Candles	Sex (too old or too young for)	Birthday card
Party	Booze (always associated with	Gift
Cake	everything)	Age (young or old)
Ice Cream	Celebrate	Money

Now let's take one of the associations, *cake,* and mentally juggle it around. Picture the cake in your mind, decorated and everything, as birthday cakes always are. See the candles on it, already lit. Let's fool with the candles for awhile. How about exaggerating the number of candles? Imagine the cake covered with so many candles that they're even on the sides of the cake. Keep going. Stick more candles into it. There! Now there are so many candles on the cake that it's impossible to get another one on. At this point, let's be silly and imagine that each candle stands for a year of the person's life. What are they going to do next year when they're another year older? There's not enough room on the cake for another candle? Guess they'll have to get a bigger cake or put on a lot less candles. Hey! Maybe we've got an idea there. Let's write that down (always get your rough ideas down on paper where you can see them [and before you forget them]. They're easier to work with that way). Our rough gag might look like this:

> You're getting to the age when you've got to
> make a decision . . .
> . . . whether to buy a lot less birthday candles or
> get a bigger birthday cake!

From the rough gag, we go to the next step, the *polishing* stage. Polishing a gag is something both the new and the professional gag writer have to do. You will get to the point, professionally, where you can kick a gag around mentally and put it down in a fairly well-polished form, but don't worry about trying it now. When you get to that level of proficiency, you won't have to make a point of doing it, it will just happen.

The polishing stage is the stage where you play with words — literally. You take your rough gag and you heighten its comic effect by substituting one word that more accurately describes what you had said before in six; you transpose words and phrases, you tear the gag apart, build it and reshape it with words until you have the tightest, strongest, briefest, and funniest copy possible, a strong, solid lead-in with a real zinger of a punchline! Let's polish.

The lead-in of our gag now reads:

> You're getting to the age when you've got to
> make a decision . . .

Start with that. One of the best ways to tighten up a gag and make it better and funnier is to make it as short as possible. There are times, of course, when you might want to add a word or more to heighten the comic effect of a gag, but, in general, the briefer the gag the better. Let's see how we might shorten our lead-in.

How about changing

> You're *getting to* the age . . .

to

> You've *reached* the age . . .

We've not only shortened the lead-in by one word, but we've made it more definite because ". . . getting to the age . . ." means that the person is not yet at the age but will be soon, while ". . . reached the age . . ." means that the person is at that age *now*, which ties in better with the whole premise of our gag.

Now let's take our whole lead-in

> You've reached the age when it's time to
> make a decision . . .

and change it to read:

> You've reached the age where it's time to
> make a great decision . . .

Here we've done two things: We've changed "when" to "where" because *where* denotes a situation or circumstances, which is what we want to imply here; and we've added the word *great* to *decision* to give it more importance and impact. We want to do this because our punchline is going to define the *great decision,* so we want to make it stand out as much as possible.

Now how about the punchline? What is our *great decision?* In our rough form we said:

> . . . whether to buy a lot less birthday candles
> or get a bigger birthday cake!

Well, it does explain our great decision, but it's awfully wordy and very un-punchy. So let's see if we can tighten it up.

How about changing the first part

> . . . whether to buy a lot less birthday candles . . .

to simply

> . . . fewer candles . . .

Everyone knows that *somebody* has to *buy* the candles, they're not given away, so there is no reason to spell it out! Thus we can delete the words *whether to buy*. Next, *fewer* has basically the same meaning as *a lot less* and saves us two words. And since we've talked about *age* in our lead-in, we've established that it's a *birthday* gag, so why use the word *birthday* in our punchline? What other kind of candles would they be? Following this latter thought through means we can also get rid of the word *birthday* in the last part of our punchline. So it will change that from

> . . . or get a bigger birthday cake!

to

> . . . or get a bigger cake!

And since we knocked out the word *buy,* we can also knock out the word *get* for the same reason. Altogether we've knocked out several superfluous and repetitious words and we've come up with a tighter and stronger gag, which looks like this in its final, polished version:

> You've reached the age where it's time to make
> a great decision . . .
> . . . fewer candles or a bigger cake!

Go back and compare our polished version to our original rough gag; notice the tremendous improvement we've made in it. This is the type of thing you should try to do with every one of your ideas before you send them out; get them down into the tightest, most polished form possible, that will improve your material almost more than anything else you can do.

Humor method: *Characteristics.*

Again, let's work on a studio birthday card. In this method we take some of the characteristics of a person who is having a birthday, or perhaps we should say, of a person who is getting older. Most of them we can relate to ourselves. Let's list a few:

Old age	Youthful appearance
Bulging midriff	Ballooning bottom
Lack of energy	Trying to stay in shape
Wrinkles	Sex urge on the downswing
Older generation	Tire easily

Let's kick of couple of these around until we come up with some humorous slants and get them down on paper. How about *trying to stay in shape?!* Wait a minute! Isn't there something about being ship-shape? Might be an idea there. Let's go back to our *association* method for a moment and see if we can come up with something connected to *ship-shape.*

Shipe-shape	Poop deck	Mizzen mast
Barnacles	Main mast	Ladder
Clean	Bilge	Head
Porthole	Stern	Bow

Picking *bilge* out of this list, and going back to our *characteristics,* it looks like we might be able to work up a play-on-words with *bulging midriff* by leaving the midriff off and coming up with something like *bulging bilge.* Maybe "A bulging bilge won't hurt anything!" Let's tie this to our *ship-shape* thought and come up with a rough gag something like this:

Have a Happy Birthday, and don't let yourself worry about not being in ship-shape . . .
. . . a bulging bilge won't hurt anything!

Now let's polish. *Have a Happy Birthday* sounds okay, but

what about *don't let yourself worry about not being in ship-shape?* It's too indirect, too passive . . . let's make it more direct, more positive. How about *don't worry about being ship-shape?* (Notice what happened to the number of words when we went to a direct statement.) That sounds pretty good! So our lead-in will now read:

> Have a Happy Birthday and don't worry about
> being ship-shape . . .

Now we'll polish the punchline. *A bulging bilge never hurt anything!* Not too pointed. Maybe it should be *A bulging bilge never hurt anyone!* The *anyone* sounds more like it. Now, wouldn't it be a little cuter and have a certain balance and swing to it if we would reverse *bulging bilge* and make it into *a little bulge in the bilge?!* Right? Right! So now here is our polished version:

> Have a Happy Birthday, and don't worry about
> being ship-shape . . .
> . . . a little bulge in the bilge never hurt
> anyone!

That sounds pretty good. And while we're on this ship-shape kick, let's go back again to that association list and pull out *poopdeck.* Don't know if you noticed, but we've got a Get Well card there. I've already polished the gag and put it down, but I'm not going to give you my polished version yet, just the rough gag. You work at polishing it, and then somewhere later in this chapter I'll give you my polished version to compare with yours. Here's the rough gag:

> Hope it won't be long before you'll really
> be feeling ship-shape again . . .
> . . . there is never anything worse than having
> a pooped deck!

By the way, you'll find that what just happened . . . having one gag lead to another . . . will occur frequently. Sometimes you'll get a whole string of gags that way. With that one premise alone — *ship-shape* — you could really, if you'll pardon the expression, go overboard!

Humor method!: *Switching.*

Switching means taking an existing gag and altering it, rephrasing it, cleaning it up, or making it more risque, modernizing it, changing and twisting it in some manner so that it becomes a wholly new and different gag. Switching can provide you with more material than any other humor method. You should practice it constantly with every gag you read. How is it done?

You can take the basic lead-in and change the punchline:

> Happy Birthday, and don't worry about being
> ship-shape . . .
> . . . a few barnacles on your bottom doesn't
> mean you're ready for dry dock!

You can take the basic punchline and change the lead-in:

> On your birthday, don't worry if you're beginning
> to look like a waterlogged ship . . .
> . . . a little bulge in the bilge never hurt
> anyone!

You can retain the premise of the gag and write a new version of it:

> Have a Happy Birthday and don't worry if you
> can't run like an athlete . . .
> . . . a little jig when you jog won't hurt you!

Retaining the premise of a gag and writing a new version of it is probably the best method of switching. It will give your ideas more freshness and originality, and at the same time insure that you are not staying too close to the original gag. Just for kicks, here are three versions of the same premise of a non-greeting card gag. Try writing some of your own.

Original gag:

> COMIC: I love the way those southern girls talk . . .
> by the time they tell you about their past
> you're part of it.

Switched gag:

> COMIC: I love the slow way those southern girls talk . . .
> you ask one of them to say *yes,* and by the time
> she says *no,* it's too late!

Switched gag:

> GIRL: I've just got to learn to talk faster . . . the
> other night that salesman fellow asked me if I
> would, and by the time I said no, I had!

A lot of switchable material can be garnered from published greeting cards, magazine cartoons, advertising slogans and promotions, joke books, humorous dictionaries, and whatever word-of-mouth jokes may be popular. Of all of these sources, published greeting cards are probably the best and most logical source of greeting card gags. They already contain all the necessary ingredients: me-to-you message, humor, sentiment, etc. You cannot, of course, lift a gag word for word, you must switch it into a new version of the original gag.

Sometimes just reading through a handful of cards can be a big help in priming your humorous well, even without your doing any actual switching. The cards get your mind thinking in a greeting card vein. The thoughts that run through your mind as you read over the already published cards can give birth to one, or maybe two or three new gags that are not really from any one card, but are really the combination of ideas created in your mind from several of the cards. Just one word in the copy may set you off on a new line of thinking where you may eventually be rewarded with a salable gag.

In addition to greeting cards, magazine cartoons can be fertile soil for switching, or for that matter getting completely new ideas. In a cartoon you have before you a visual humorous image as well as humorous copy. The characters themselves, or what they are doing or wearing, may give you a completely new idea that you can slant toward the card markets.

After the humor *methods*, namely, *Association, Characteristics,* and *Switching,* come the humor *formulas.* Here are the ones you will use most often, one at a time.

Humor formula: *Exaggeration.*

There are probably more gags written using *exaggeration* than there are using any of the other formulas. As you become familiar with it, you'll spot it often in all types of humor.

When using the exaggeration formula, you do exactly what the word says; you exaggerate, but *wildly,* almost beyond belief, far enough so that there is humor in the exaggeration itself, but also so that there is no possibility that the exaggeration could be true. Example:

> A year ago I bought you a birthday card and
> here it is time for another one already . . .
> . . . knowing you is getting to be darn expensive!

(Here we're exaggerating how expensive a quarter a year is.) Now this one:

> Your birthday is a perfect time to have all your
> friends and relatives gather around you . . .
> . . . to help blow out all those candles!

(Here we're exaggerating the number of candles to the point that it would take a lot of people to blow them all out.)

A great practice for writing exaggeration gags is to take some kind of a premise and swing off on it, even a non-greeting card premise is beautiful for practice. For example: *My girl friend* (or *boy friend*) *is so thin . . .*

> My girl friend is so thin she keeps getting her
> foot caught in sidewalk cracks!
>
> My girl friend is so thin if it wasn't for her
> belly button she wouldn't have any curves at all!
>
> My girl friend is so thin she looks like half a
> railroad track!

Let's try another premise just for kicks. Like: *The bride was
so young . . .*

> The bride was so young her father didn't give
> her away, her baby sitter did!
>
> The bride was so young her friends didn't throw
> rice, they threw Pablum!
>
> The bride was so young, instead of the minister asking
> her to say "I do," he burped her!

Or we can take a premise nearer the greeting card line. Like:
I know someone who is so sick . . .

> I know someone who is so sick Excedrin gives
> him a headache! (or . . . Anacin makes him nervous; or . . .
> Alka Seltzer gives him the blahs.)

Try some premises of your own using the exaggeration formula.
They're great practice.

Humor formula: *Insult.*

The *insult* formula is self-explanatory. Be careful with it and
don't spend too much time writing insulting — better known as
slam — greeting cards. About the only cards they are used in
right now are Valentines, and even there they are used sparsely.
Here are a couple of examples of them:

> Valentine, anyone who takes you for a fool . . .
> . . . makes no mistake!
>
> Happy Valentine's Day to tall, dark, and . . .
> . . . hands!

Above all, don't get the old idea, which has lingered from the first studio cards, that *all* studio cards are of the insult variety. Very, very few are.

Humor formula: *Reverse.*

The reverse formula *reverses* the familiar or expected order and direction of things. It exchanges the unexpected for the expected. As an example, a simple reverse joke would be *Did you hear about the flea who was so rich he went out and bought himself a dog?* In greeting cards, reverse formula gags would come out like this:

> Before I met you, I wanted to be against everything . . .
> ، . . now I just want to be against you!

> Just because I want to hug and kiss you all the
> time, it doesn't mean you have to be my
> Valentine . . .
> . . . you can be my pet grapefruit!!!

The reverse formula joke might also be called the juxtaposition or double-cross joke in that you lead your reader into expecting one thing and you then double-cross him by giving him something else. It's one of the most effective and laugh provoking formulas there is. Use it often.

Humor formula: *Combinations.*

In a *combination* formula joke you combine two normally unrelated things into a funny thought or image that contains some element of both things. It's a wacky formula, and can produce some delightful and wacky gags. For instance:

> Wanted to send you something special for Easter,
> so I crossed a rabbit with a piece of lead . . .
> . . . would you be interested in a repeating pencil!?

> Wanted to send a special singing telegram to you for
> your birthday, so I crossed a parrot with a gorilla . . .
> . . . when it sings "Happy Birthday" to you, you
> better listen!!!

Humor formula: *Definition.*

This is Bob Hope's favorite type of gag. He tells them something like this: "I just flew in from California. You know what California is: It's the land of the freeway and the home of the knave." In greeting cards, definition formula gags would go something like this one:

> Valentine, do you know the difference between a
> hamburger and sex?? . . . You don't!!??
> . . . meet me for lunch tomorrow!!!

Humor formula: *Misunderstanding.*

In the misunderstanding formula joke, the punchline seems to say "I wasn't talking about what you thought I was talking about. You misunderstood me." Notice in these two examples how the punchline changes the meaning of the lead-in.

> To someone in the service: For your birthday, I
> wanted to send you a genuine, American-made, foxhole
> warmer . . .
> . . . but the postmaster said I weighed too much to mail!

> To help celebrate your birthday, I'm sending over
> a huge dry martini! . . .
> . . . Giuseppe Martini! . . . he hasn't touched a drop
> in twenty years!

Humor formula: *Literal (truth).*

In this formula, you use the literal or true meaning of the main word in your lead-in. It is often a word that has a double meaning, or that can mean different things depending on the tone and inflection used with it. Here are a couple of examples:

> Valentine, I'll *teach* you to fool around with
> me! . . .
> . . . when do you want your first *lesson?!*

> Valentine, I've got enough love for *two!* . . .
> . . . bring a friend!

The literal formula also plays upon the true reason for something occurring. For example:

> People our age have 23% fewer cavities . . .
> . . . of course, we have 23% fewer teeth!

Humor formula: *Play-On-Words.*

In this type of gag you do just exactly what the formula says: *play* with words. They can be foolish words, words that sound almost alike, words that can be given a meaning different than any that was ever intended for them, words misused, and any other word trick you can think of. Here are a couple of examples:

> Wish I could think of the right spell . . .
> . . . so I could "betwitch" you on Halloween!

> Have a Happy Birthday, and don't worry . . .
> you're not getting old until you've got a
> GO-GO mind . . .
> . . . and a CAN'T-CAN'T body!!!

Humor formula: *Repetition.*

In the repetition formula joke you repeat in the punchline a key word or phrase that appears in the lead-in, usually changing or expanding its meaning to give the comic effect. Here's an example:

> Have a Happy Birthday and don't worry about
> your *declining* years . . .
> . . . until you start *declining* booze, parties
> and sex!

Humor formula: *Whimsy.*

In this formula, the humor comes from inconsistency and there is almost always no definite punchline. The gag simply follows a humorous turn of the mind, and the punchline seldom seems to have anything at all to do with what was in the lead-in, or, at least, not very much to do with it. Example:

> I like you . . .
> . . . you're nicer than warm sheets in January.

Humor formula: *Topical.*

In this formula you use anything that is currently in the news — ad slogans, political slogans, phrases, hip words, well-known personalities. Here's one:

> Fun goes better with . . .
> Food goes better with . . .
> Things go better with . . .
> . . . YOU!

Look around you and see what is currently making a splash of any kind, anything at all in any field, and see if you can't twist it into a topical greeting card. Here's another one:

> Valentine, I may not be the world's greatest
> lover . . .
> . . . but I give trading stamps!

Humor formula: *Zany.*

This formula is the most fun of all because it's wild, irrational, fantastic, carefree, ridiculous. It doesn't tie you down to a thing! The formula is closely related to the *exaggeration* formula, but the gags in it are seldom rooted in reality. The gags are just like that silly feeling you get that you want to dance in the middle of the street for no darn reason at all. The master exponent of the *zany* gag is the Big Daddy of Us All, Jonathan Winters. He's the total master, there ain't none better! For an example of zany humor, reread the first paragraph of this chapter, and these two greeting card ideas.

> Last night I had a dream about you and I woke
> up with a strange ringing in my ear . . .
> . . . but nobody answered so I went back to
> sleep!

I hope you have a Happy Thanksgiving . . . but
don't do like Percy Fairweather did last year.
Percy ate so much he got bigger and bigger and
bigger . . .
. . . and blew out his belly button!!!

I have now emptied my bag of the methods and formulas for getting funny ideas when you're alone, save for one! My own personal method, my own personal formula! And since you've been so kind and patient and have read to the end of this chapter, I cannot in all good conscience, hold out on you. Here it is.

You lie on a tiger-skin rug in front of a roaring fireplace reading the latest unexpurgated edition of *Alice in Wonderland* to a . . .

P.S. Here's my polished version of the gag we talked about way back when:

Hope you'll soon be ship-shape again . . .
. . . there's nothing worse than a pooped-deck!

How does it compare with yours?

Chapter XVII

Getting Your Ideas Ready for Sale

by H. Joseph Chadwick

Now that you have your ideas written, and they're fresh and original and timely and all the things they should be, it's simply a matter of tossing them into an envelope and bundling them off to some eagerly awaiting editor. Right? Wrong!

Just as you don't simply "dash off" some writing on a piece of paper, neither do you simply "send it off" in the mail. The way you prepare and submit your ideas is as important as the writing itself because it can mean the difference between rejections and sales. So let's get busy and learn the things we have to know about *marketing* our ideas.

One of the first things to consider is the idea itself. *Is it ready for market?* Here is a list of some things to check for (the check-list includes items you would check for only in specific types of cards, such as studio or conventional. Use each item accordingly):

1. *Does the idea have a me-to-you message?* This is the basic, essential ingredient in any greeting card. It gives the reason for sending the card: because you want to say something to the person you are sending the card to. You might say it formally, sentimentally, amusingly, informally, or hilariously; but however you say it, the me-to-you message is the reason you or anyone else sends a greeting card.

It is possible to get away occasionally with a joke gag that doesn't have a me-to-you message in a studio card, but it is a rare bird even there and best avoided until your feet are not only wet, but soaked.

2. *Is the idea relevant to the occasion?* This means: Is the subject matter in your idea normally associated with the occasion? For example, cake for birthdays, thermometer for get wells, celebrating for anniversaries, Santa Claus for Christmas, and like so. Here are some subjects that are *not* relevant to the occasion: drinking for Halloween or Easter, trick or treat for birthdays, gifts for Thanksgiving, risque gags for Bar Mitzvah, and so on. The more relevant your idea is to the occasion, the better are your chances of selling it.

3. *Does your idea use a phony situation?* Here is an example of one:

> When you chased your nurse around your bed
> last night, it proved one thing . . .
> . . . you've taken a turn for the nurse!

Obviously, the patient did not chase the nurse around the bed — unless the patient was a male editor, because you know how they are — so this is an attempt to set up a phony situation in order to get to a punchline. When the gag is a good one, and you resort to a phony situation, it simply means you haven't worked the idea out properly. Put it aside for awhile and then try it again later, but don't send it out until it's right and logical within its premise.

4. *Is the idea generally sendable? Who will send it? To whom?* Many ideas submitted for cards are good gags, but just aren't usable as greeting cards. For example:

> A bachelor is a man who doesn't have to
> wash a dish . . .
> . . . until he wants to eat from one!

Now this might be useful as an epigram in a magazine, but it's no greeting card. And to those of you who say you could obviously send this idea to a bachelor friend, I'll agree with you, you could, but why would you?

Or as another example, the idea might be one that has to be sent to a man by a woman, but is too risque for a woman to ever buy it. So although a lot of male editors might fall off their editorial chairs laughing, they won't pay you a cent for your gag and all you've managed to do is bring a little sunlight into their bleak lives, which might gain you a few lifelong friends but won't put any money into your pocket.

Check your idea carefully and make certain it is as generally sendable as you can make it. One good check is to try to think of a couple of people you know who could send the card or who could receive it. Would *you send* the card? Could it be sent to you? By whom?

Another thing that will make the idea more generally sendable is to keep the personal pronoun "I" out of it. Remember, there are many cases where two or more people send a single card. If a lot of your ideas have an "I" in them, try to write it out. Your material will be improved. Here is how it might work:

> I don't want you to think of this as just
> a birthday card . . .
> . . . I want you to think of it as a present!
>
> Don't think of this as just a birthday card . . .
> . . . think of it as a present!

Notice that when you leave the "I" out, the idea often shortens, and remember that old saying: "Brevity rhymes with levity!" Which brings us to our next checklist item.

5. Is your idea as brief as possible? This doesn't mean that your idea should be short simply for the sake of being short.

There are times when you may even have to lengthen a build-up to make the punchline more effective. What it does mean is that your idea should contain no useless words, words that do not contribute to the idea. Any extra words will simply distract the reader's attention from the meat of your idea. Cut the useless words out! For example, instead of saying something like:

> Twenty-five cents is a lot more money than
> I ordinarily spend for a birthday card . . .
> . . . but all of the twenty-five cent presents
> looked cheap!

say:

> Ordinarily I don't spend 25c for a
> birthday card . . .
> . . . but the 25c presents looked cheap!

6. *Is your idea written in plain, simple language?* When writing your ideas, use ordinary, everyday language, plain, simple words that guys like me can understand. Don't say things like: *don't be disagreeably effusive,* say *don't shoot your mouth off.* And not: *terribly disheveled,* but: *messy.* Greeting cards are no place to try to be flowery or show how many big words you know . . . or try to play "Stump the editor." Because if you do stump him, he won't reach for his dictionary, he'll reach for a rejection slip.

7. *Is the idea funny?* I wish there were some simple rule of the index finger that I could give you to help you decide whether or not your idea is actually funny. But there isn't. And there never will be, at least, not until we all start laughing at the same things. But as long as one man's pun is another man's joke, it will be difficult, and at times downright impossible, to determine what is funny. The only things that will help you to tell to some degree whether or not an idea is funny is experience.

Fortunately, you don't have to wait for experience to come to you. It's available all around you in the form of greeting cards, joke books, humorous stories, comedians, television, anything and everything that contains humor. By burying yourself in all the various types of humor available to you today, you gain the benefit of the judgment of all the editors, writers, and performers responsible for the publication and showing of humorous material. Soon you will find yourself able to tell fairly well what is *amusing,* what is *funny,* and what is *hilarious.* The more humor you read and study, the more experience you will gain, and you'll soon learn to judge your own material well enough to tell whether it's as funny and punchy as it could be, or whether it needs more work. Read and listen to all the humor you can find. It's the quickest way to gain experience.

8. *Is the humor understandable?* Humor that isn't understandable can be the result of several things. It could be too subtle — the general public just isn't that sharp when it comes to humor. That's why your most popular comedians are the ones who hit you in the face with their humor. You don't have to try to figure it out, they spell it all out and let you have it wide open with no guesswork. Don't try to be subtle or cute with your humor. Make it obvious. Hit 'em in the puss with it!

Another thing that can kill greeting card humor is the use of little-known or old happenings, expressions, sayings, songs, historical events, and et ceteras that the writer assumes everyone knows because they and their friends do. We once put out a card that used the well-known expression "hair of the dog." The card died on the racks. When we checked further to find out why the card didn't sell, we discovered that only about two out of every ten people knew what that well-known expression "hair of the dog" meant. Don't work gags around old expressions or little known events or whathaveyou's that aren't a current topic. Use things that are in-the-news and popular now.

A third killer of greeting card humor is the local or "in" joke.

Basing a joke on something that is well known in Los Angeles or in New York may get you a lot of laughs in Los Angeles or in New York, but it isn't going to sell greeting cards in Burlington, Vermont, or nationally. The same goes for jokes that are only funny if you belong to the Elks, or the Knights of Columbus, or if you hang around the men's locker room at the Loyal Order of Sports. These may get great laughs among your friends, but don't try them on greeting cards because no one will understand them, and the editor will just send you a rejection slip that is very easy to understand.

What this all means is that to be funny, humor, any kind of humor, must be about things that people will recognize. It's as simple as that.

9. Is the occasion identified on the cover? Although many writers may not be aware of it, greeting cards are designed perhaps more with the buyer in mind than with the receiver. There is an old saying somewhere in the greeting card industry (What would an industry be without an old saying?) that the card design makes the buyer pick up the card, and the text sells the card. Now, since cards are usually bought for a specific occasion, card companies try to identify the occasion for which the card was written on the cover of the card, so that it will be easy for the buyer to spot the kind of card he wants from among the sometimes hundreds displayed in a rack.

The occasion can be identified in two ways. It can be identified either through design — hearts on Valentine's Day, Santa Claus and winter scenes on Christmas cards, green colors and Leprechauns on St. Patrick's Day — or, since there are no identifying colors or designs that can be used for *everyday* cards, it can be done with text. For example: *Happy Birthday to a girl who . . .* or *On your Anniversary, be sure . . .* or *Congratulations, Graduate, looks like you've . . .*

Study the cards on the racks to see the many devices editors and art directors use to identify the occasion on the cover of a card, and try to incorporate them into your own material. It will improve your ideas.

10. Would your idea result in excessive damage to the finished card on the rack? In Chapters XIII and XIV, we discussed attachments and mechanical actions that could cause rack damage to a card. If your idea uses either an action or an attachment, give it a final check to make certain you haven't unconsciously designed a card that could result in rack damage.

11. Have you worked your idea out to its best possible form? Many ideas that editors receive contain excellent subject matter that could be cutely illustrated or would make a slightly different and fresh sounding greeting card, but the idea just doesn't hold together. For example, here is an idea I received in the mail that we thought contained excellent subject matter for a Valentine's Day card.

> Next to my blanket (show small child chewing on
> blanket) . . .
> . . . you're the greatest!

One thing that appealed to the art director about this idea was the possibility of illustrating it with a small child. (Art directors are always trying to get away from the single neuter character illustration they have to use on too many cards.) But as we studied this idea, it almost completely fell apart.

First, the illustration of the child *chewing* on the blanket had no meaning in itself or any connection with the text. Second, there was no logical tie-in between the *blanket* and *greatest*. Blankets are not great or wonderful. Although the idea had a nice approach in the buildup, it fell apart in the punchline. However, as we studied the idea further, we found that a logical relationship could be established between the child and blanket and an affection-type Valentine's Day card.

Our first thought was, what meaning does a blanket have for a child that might fall within the realm of affection? Well, a blanket gives a child a sense of security. He can snuggle up to a blanket, it keeps him warm and comfortable, makes him feel safe and protected, and on and on. Using this logical approach to the writer's idea, we rewrote it and this it how it came out:

> Valentine, next to my blanket (child *snuggling*
> up to blanket) . . .
> . . . you keep me the warmest!

Now, besides the fact that you should never send an idea out until you're completely satisfied that it is in the best possible form you can put it in, another important factor is that most editors will cut the writer's pay when the idea has to be rewritten. Sometimes the cut will be almost half of the writer's regular pay.

When you're considering whether or not your idea is in its best possible form, think of the money. Nothing sharpens a writer's mind better than the thought of losing money.

12. Are you using old worn-out rhymes? Watch for rhymes like way, day, say, gay, may, play; love, above; years, tears, fears; do, you; kiss, bliss. They, and many like them, have been used too many times for too many years. Look for fresh, new rhymes, new ways to say old things. The extra time you spend could bring many extra dollars back in sales. Don't send rhymes out that are dull with triteness . . . find new rhymes that sparkle with brightness.

13. Are you using the word you? The most important word in greeting cards is *you!* The least important is *I.* If your idea has more I's than you's in it, edit them out! Get rid of them like they were the plague, that's about what they're worth to you. If your idea doesn't have a lot of useless I's in it, but it doesn't have any you's in it either, then rewrite it and stick some you's in there! If you don't think editors consider the word you important, the next time you're reading a bunch of cards, check them specifically for you's. And send me a dollar for each one you find. Remember the word: you . . . you . . . you . . . you . . . you . . . you . . . you . . .

14. Are you using positive statements? When writing studio gags, put your statements into positive form. Don't write around your subjects. Don't hesitate. Make definite, straight forward assertions. Don't say:

> Happy Valentine's Day to someone who is
> not only tall and dark, but also . . .
> . . . all hands.

say:

> Happy Valentine's Day to tall, dark . . .
> . . . and hands.

Use *not* for denial, never for evasion.

Now that you've checked your idea out thoroughly and feel that it's definitely ready for market, you have to decide what form to send it on. There are several basic forms used.

One form is to type the idea or verse out on a 3 x 5 or 4 x 6 card as shown below:

```
            FRONT OF CARD
    Now that you're older, remember that if
    you neck, drink, and stay out late . . . men
    will call you FAST . . .
    . . . just as FAST as they can get a
    phone !
               Happy Birthday


             BACK OF CARD
    Name                      Idea code number
    Address
```

These flat cards are a submission form that you can use for ideas for all greeting cards, conventional, inspirational, informal, juvenile, humorous, and studio, and also for ideas for mottos, buttons, and stationery.

Another form you can use for studio and humorous cards is simple folded sheets of paper, ranging from folded 4 x 6 sheets to actual card size. The buildup is then typed or neatly hand-printed on the outside cover of the folded paper, and the punch-line is put on the right inside page. For studio and humorous card ideas, this outside/inside form of presentation is much more effective than the flat card because it hides the punchline until the buildup has been read, thus ensuring that the surprise ending of the gag has been retained.

There are, however, some editors who insist that you submit all your ideas on 3 x 5 cards. For them, regardless of your personal feelings or preference, you must send your ideas in on the form they want. Personally, if the pay rate was high enough, I would send ideas to them on the back of a camel, front or rear hump, if that is what it took to sell them.

The third form of submission, used basically for studio, humorous, and juvenile cards, is to make up a complete rough *dummy* that is as close to the finished card as you can visualize it. This includes everything called for in the finished card: actual size, rough sketch, attachmen, mechanical action, unusual folds, french folds, cutouts, color, etc. This is the best form of the three for the cards mentioned above, and is the one most used by professional free-lance writers. It is also one that anyone can learn to use regardless of *original* drawing ability.

If you're interested in completely designing a greeting card, or even in becoming a professional greeting card artist, — a talent you can wed to your writing ability — there are hundreds of excellent books, courses, and schools for artists available today. Being able to draw enables a writer to do many *visual* gags that he cannot do if he can only write. (A visual gag is one in which most, if not all, of the humor depends upon the drawing or series of drawings used in the card, similar to captionless cartoons. Check cards on the racks for the visual gag type.)

If you only want to learn to sketch well enough to illustrate your idea, make it understandable and perhaps enhance it somewhat, then the easiest way is to buy a bunch of cards that have characters on them that express the basic emotions like anger, shyness, love, laughter, happiness, sorrow, etc., and then learn to draw variations of these characters in various positions. For *get well* ideas, buy cards with hospital beds, doctors, nurses, and medical equipment illustrated on them. For Valentine ideas, cupids, bows and arrows, hearts, and so forth. Same principle for any other type of ideas. Use the same characters and basic equipments on any of the ideas you want to illustrate. Using this method, you'll soon learn to do a professional looking job illustrating any of your ideas.

One further thing: If you don't sketch at all, and don't want or have the time to learn, don't waste your time giving a word-picture of what kind of illustration you think the card should have, unless the illustration is essential to your idea. With that one exception, I can't think of any case where the suggested illustration was used in the final design of the card. Let's face it, writers who cannot even sketch can't possibly come up with as good a design as professional designers, so why should they even try?

If the illustration is an *essential* part of your idea, then, of course, suggest it. For example, in this studio card idea the illustration is part of the gag:

> (Devil blowing horn, musical note coming
> out of horn; along with note, like on
> a sheet of music, are two words:) You're
> sick? . . .
> . . . that's a helluva note!

In this next card idea, the illustration is not essential to the gag and so no word-picture is needed, and none should be given!

> Just because I'd like to squeeze you
> and squeeze you, it doesn't mean you
> have to be my Valentine . . .
> . . . you can be my pet grapefruit!!!

Giving a word-picture when an illustration isn't essential to your gag just wastes your time, clutters up your form with a lot of glump, and distracts the editor's attention away from the gag itself. Better to spend your time writing more of those $50 gags you're so good at.

Regardless of which form you use to present your ideas, don't clutter up the front of them with routine information like your name, address, and code number. Put all of this information on the back of your form where it's out of the way until the editor needs to refer to it. And don't waste time typing or writing your name over and over. For about $3.00 at most stationery stores you can buy a rubber stamp with your name and address. It will save you hours of time, time you could be using to write ideas, and the sale of just one of those ideas could more than pay for the stamp. To change the old saying: *Don't be penny wise and time foolish!*

At this point, you've checked your ideas out thoroughly and they are all ready for submission. But not quite. There are still a lot of do's and don'ts to consider before sealing your envelope.

Make certain your name, complete address, and code number are on the back of *each* form.

Be sure your envelopes are large enough to hold your ideas. For full-size dummies, invest in heavyweight manila envelopes, available at most department and stationery stores. They come in all the convenient sizes, and though they cost a little more than regular envelopes, they are well worth the price.

Above all, don't *squeeze* your ideas into an envelope. There's nothing more annoying than trying to tear open an envelope that is crammed so full you can't even get hold of a corner of it. And don't send a return envelope that is too small to put your rejected ideas into. If that sounds silly, it is! But it happens almost every day. Why do writers do it? Beats me. Either they don't bother checking the size of their return envelope, or they have the strange idea that if the editor can't get their ideas into their return envelope, he'll buy them! And they're mistaken, of course, because we usually manage to get their ideas into their too small return envelope!

Don't use paper clips to hold your ideas together. Paper clips make marks on the cards or dummies and you have to redo them after only two or three submissions. Use rubber bands instead, and make sure the bands are large enough to hold the ideas firmly yet not cut into the paper.

Don't clip the stamps to your return envelope. There has never been a time yet when every idea from a batch has been bought, so you're bound to have returns. Consequently, your return envelope is going to be used and it is going to need stamps. Use the glue on the stamps for what it was intended, to stick the stamps to your return envelope.

It would probably pay you to invest in a postage scale. Most department and stationery stores sell them for about $3.00. This way you'll be sure of having the right number of stamps on your envelopes so you won't be wasting money. And don't forget that you can buy 1st class stamps in rolls of 100, and get a plastic stamp dispenser for the roll for about 5¢, both at the Post Office. Both are great time savers.

One question that always seems to arise is whether or not to include a letter with your submissions. It's a question that may never be settled, but here's my opinion of it.

If you have something to say that is *pertinent* to your material, then by all means include a letter with your submissions.

But do *not* include a letter simply to tell the editor that you are submitting ideas to him. He can see that. Or to list the ideas you are submitting to him. He's not going to check your list. Or to tell him you're just beginning and you would appreciate his considering your ideas. He's being paid to consider *all* ideas, and telling him you're just beginning is likely to put a couple of strikes against you, especially if he's had a hectic day, or a couple of new writers have just accused him of everything from plagiarism to child molesting. Besides, you're doing all this study and work and practice so you won't be or look like a new writer, so why tell the editor you're a new writer when you look like a professional? Let your ideas speak for themselves.

Above all, don't tell the editor that your ideas are for sale at his usual rates, or for $2.00 apiece as one writer told me, or that you're selling all rights, or North American Serial rights only, or that you'll sell your ideas only on a royalty basis. (One writer wrote me that he would sell his idea, one only, written on a piece of scrap paper so I could hardly read it, for 1¢ on each card for the first 5,000 printed, 1½¢ on all over 5,000, with a minimum printing of 15,000 cards, and I had exactly 10 days in which to reply or he would withdraw his offer. Would you be surprised if I told you I turned his offer down?)

First, greeting card companies buy *all rights*. Second, editors go out of their way to pay fair prices to their writers, but their rates are normally fixed for certain types of ideas, so *all* writers get the usual rates. This is not to say that writers who sell an editor regularly cannot get higher than normal rates. They can, and usually do. But writers who are just beginning to sell an editor, or who sell him only occasionally, get the normal fixed rates. Third, unless you're a well-known writer, poet, cartoonist, or artist, it's 99½ percent against your getting royalties for a greeting card idea. If you insist on royalties when you don't deserve them, the editor will insist on sending you a rejection slip that you do deserve. Get famous first, then worry about royalties.

Finally, remember one thing: you are never wrong in *not* including a letter with your submissions, but saying anything wrong in one can kill a sale. If you're uncertain about whether or not to include a letter and what to say, perhaps the best rule of the little finger is: *When in doubt . . . leave it out!*

Since you're in this business to make money, it makes sense to get as much for your writing as you possibly can, so, in general, send your material to the highest paying market first. Then to the next highest paying market, and so on down the list. This is for everyday material. Seasonal material has to be sent as the editors ask for it, since most editors, but not all, will look at seasonal ideas only at certain times of the year. Ask the editor periodically what seasonal line he will be looking at next and when he will start looking.

Ordinarily, send between 10 and 15 ideas in each batch. Less than 10 wastes your time and postage, and more than 15 overwhelms the editor, who might tend to give less of a reading to each idea.

Never address your envelope directly to the company. If you do not know the name of the editor, then address your envelope to the type of editor for whom your ideas are intended: humorous editor, studio editor, conventional editor, juvenile editor, weird editor, and like so. If you do not, then the company mailroom must open your envelope to find out where it's suppose to go and even what's in it, which could result in some of your ideas getting lost, or being cut by the electric openers most companies now use. In addition, the extra handling causes the company added expense which doesn't help your cause any.

To sell, you must submit; to sell a lot, you must submit a lot. Keep as many ideas as you can in the mail. For part-time writers, this should be in the area of 500 ideas. For full-time writers, 1,000 ideas should be a bare minimum. These figures will vary, of course, during times when the return mail is heavy, and when many companies are asking for seasonal ideas. But they are reasonable figures to shoot for. One top writer I know keeps approximately 3,000 ideas in the mail at all times. He also writes light verse and humor pieces. How does he do it? Well, I'll have to admit that he does have a secret, as do all successful writers. He keeps writing!

Remember, you know how to write, you know the techniques used to write sentiment and humor, you know everything necessary to sit at your typewriter and start writing. You don't have to wait for the mood to strike you. You can sit down and write any time you want to, and even when you don't want to, but have to. The only mood writers there are, are those who haven't properly learned all the techniques of writing, and are too lazy or lacking in ambition to learn them.

And if you say that's a lot of hogwash, that a true writer can only write when the so-called *muse* is on him, then you're forgetting the thousands of newspaper, television, radio, industrial, greeting card, public relations, advertisement, and magazine writers and editors who write *on demand* day after day and year after year. If they can do it, so can you. Don't mistake laziness for a lack of the muse; there tain't no such animal!

Once you get your ideas out in the mail, don't sit around and wait impatiently for them to come back. You can't pray your ideas into selling. The only thing that is going to bring a constant *inflow* of checks is a constant *outflow* of ideas. Spend your time working and writing, not waiting and wishing.

If, when you get your rejects back, there is a note from the editor telling you that he has an idea similar to one of yours already in his line, don't panic. He's not accusing you of copying the idea or trying to steal it from his company. He is simply letting you know that he already has one like yours so that if you spot it on the racks six months hence you won't accuse *him* of stealing it from *you*.

Now, what do you do about it? Well, if he simply says that the idea is similar to one he already has, he's probably just talking about the basic premise of the gag, and so you're safe in continuing to submit it to other companies. If, however, he says your idea is identical with, or exactly like, a card his company already has out or that he just bought from another writer, or words to that effect (He may even send you a copy of his company's card so you can see how close it is to your idea), then you would probably be better off destroying your form and not taking a chance on it. Some writers make it a practice either to send the editor their destroyed idea or to tell him that they have destroyed it, and to thank him for letting them know about the duplication. They feel that this way it lets the editor know that they did not copy his company's card but had simply and honestly written an idea like it, which frequently happens. In general, it's probably a good practice to include such a note with your next submission to the editor. He may be curious about what you did with the idea, and he'll undoubtedly appreciate your thanking him. I don't see any way such a note could hurt you, and it very well might help you in the future.

Never stop submitting an idea as long as you feel it's a good one. When I was a free-lance writer, I once sold an idea on its 28th submission. Another writer I know sold an idea five years and 45 submissions after he wrote it, to an editor who had rejected it three times previously. This happens in all kinds of writing, but particularly in greeting card writing. Humor and sentiment are constantly changing things, and what was tearfully sentimental ten years ago may be corny today. The type of humor that no one thought funny last year may be considered hilarious next year. In addition, the editors may have only rejected your idea because, even though it was a good one, they had no place for it in their lines. An editor might buy a couple of fisherman birthday gags for his idea bank, but after he has a reserve of this theme, he probably won't buy another fisherman gag unless it's the greatest thing that ever came down the pike until he uses up his reserve. Your fisherman gag that you've kept circulating might get to him next year just at the time he decides it's time to buy another fisherman idea.

Another thing that will keep an editor from buying a fairly good idea is Ye Olde Budget. Most greeting card editors have only so much money that they can spend for free-lance ideas, and when the money begins to run short they often pass up ideas that they wish they could have bought. Sometimes, if their budget is looser then, they'll grab the idea on it's second time around. This type of thing very often happens with seasonal ideas. Many times I've bought Christmas ideas that I had had to pass up the previous year because of budget problems.

Remember, that each company has its own special requirements, likes, and dislikes. What won't sell to one company may often sell to another company. When I was in the free-lance business I occasionally had ideas rejected by companies who pay $10 an idea, and turned around and sold them to companies who pay $25 or more an idea.

Editors change frequently in the greeting card business, so it's possible that a company where your idea was once rejected might have a new editor who is just crazy about your kind of humor. Keep your ideas moving. They won't sell sitting in your file or in a box.

If you are submitting to a new editor or to one you've never submitted to before, and you don't know his requirements, likes or dislikes, don't send him limited captions like birth, wedding, trip, or seasonal ideas. Send him some good everyday captions! These give you your greatest possibilities for sales, especially to new editors or with first time submissions to a company.

There are, naturally, other things that you should perhaps do or not do, but you'll learn them as you go along.

Another thing you'll learn is that submitting ideas becomes quite a personal thing after awhile. Some editors you'll become very friendly with, and you'll exchange ideas and news and generally chat through the mails. If you've sold them a few things and have established good relations with them, you may even call them on the phone, or they you. Or drop in and see them if you happen to be where their plant is. You may even have lunch together. *You* buy, of course! (Only kidding . . . unless *I'm* the editor!) Or you may get to meet them at the Stationery Show that is held annually in New York City, usually in May. Many editors, art directors, creative directors, writers, and publishers attend it.

Other editors, no matter how hard you try, will remain aloof and isolated. And even though you may sell ideas to them, you simply can't reach them on a friendly basis . They're never your enemies, but they're never your friends either.

All in all submitting your material is an exciting part of the business. You'll reach the heights when your ideas are accepted, and you'll reach the bottoms when they are rejected. But, whichever way it is, it sure makes your mail a lot more exciting than getting letters from Aunt Agnes and Uncle The Ralph.

Chapter XVIII

Keeping The Record Straight

by H. Joseph Chadwick

Although most writers dislike even the thought of it, one of the most important parts of your free-lance writing is keeping records of your material: where it is, where it has been, what has sold, what is available for submitting, what has been out too long, and a dozen other minor and major things. Along with the obvious importance of keeping records, it is also important that you don't spend too much time on this one part of your writing and thereby take time away from the actual creation of ideas. With this in mind, this chapter offers you quick and simple methods of keeping records. You may already have methods that suit you to a T, and if so, stay with them, but for those of you who do not, these are practical, usable methods that will work for you *now*. You may want to change or adapt them to your own personal likes and dislikes as you progress in your writing, and this is only normal since there is really no *one best* method of record keeping, but, in the meantime, try these.

Coding Your Ideas. Because your greeting card ideas do not have titles as stories do, you should assign a code number to each idea. This makes it easy for the editor to refer to your idea, both in his correspondence with you and on all those checks he'll be sending you.

There are three basic ways of coding an idea. The first is a simple numerical code in which you number your ideas in sequence, such as 1, 2, 3, 4, or 101, 102, 103, etc. Some writers prefix the number with one or more letters that stand for the type of idea it is; for example, B for *birthdays,* GW for *get wells,* A for *anniversaries,* and like so. So a *birthday* idea might be numbered B-1234, a *get well* GW-2345, and an *anniversary* A-132. The basic problem with this method it that it is necessary to keep track somewhat of the last number you used so that you can continue numbering your ideas in sequence. Some writers don't like this coding system, because they feel an editor can tell an old idea because of the low number it might have in relation to the other ideas in the batch.

The second method is to number the ideas by *batch* or *set.* In this method, the set of ideas is given an arbitrary number like A25-. The first card in the set is then numbered A25-1, the second card A25-2, the third card A25-3, and so on. If card number A25-2 is sold, then a new idea is put into its place and given the number A25-2. Thus the cards can be kept track of by *sets.*

The third method, and the one I used to use, is an alphabetical code. The code is derived by using the first letter of the first three words in the main part of your idea (the *main* part being that part after standard opening like *For your birthday . . .* or *Because it's your birthday),* These three letters are then coupled with the letters standing for the type of idea it is. For example, if the idea started out *I know that your birthday . . .,* we would take the first letter from each of the words *I know that,* put a B in front of it and come up with B-IKT, and that would be the code number of our idea. An idea that started *No wonder you're sick,* would be coded GW-NWY. And one that started *Have an Anniversary . . .* would be coded A-HAA. This, I believe, is the fastest and easiest coding method because it can be done while you're making up your dummy or card for submission, and it isn't necessary to keep track of the last code you used because they have no reference to each other.

Regardless of which method you use, don't number every idea you write since you will be writing many more ideas than you will actually be submitting. Only number your ideas when you have them ready for submission. And don't forget to put the some code number on your file copy of the idea.

Keeping Track of Where Your Ideas Have Been. For each idea you submit, make up a 3 x 5 file card. Put the code number of the idea on the front of the card along with the idea itself. On the back of the card, record where you're sending the idea. The simpler the method of recording, the better, because it saves time. Always abbreviate the name of the company. For example: B for Barker, RC for Rust Craft, G for Gibson, V for Vagabond, BC for Buzza-Cardozo, and so on down your submission list,

The first item on the back of your card should include the company, the month, and the year. Like this: B9-68. This means the idea went first to Barker in September of 1968. The next time it goes out, simply put the company down if it is still the same month. If it is the next month or later, put down both the company and the new month. Don't put down the year until the year changes. If some editor holds the idea or comments on it, note this next to the company when the idea comes back. When you sell the idea, record the actual date of sale, and the purchase price. A short record on the back of your card might look like this:

B9-68
RC — Held 9/20/68. Ret. 10/12/68
A10
BC11 — Liked idea, no place for it.
RS
G12
V1-69 — Sold 1/13/69 — $10.

When the idea is sold, put the file card into a *sold* file under the company it was sold to. This makes it easy to refer to any idea bought by a particular company and also makes a handy reference file of the kind of ideas that company has been buying from you.

Keeping Track of Ideas You Are Submitting. Put the file cards of ideas you are submitting to one company together; then take another card and type on it the name of the company, the number of ideas in the batch, and the date the batch was mailed. Since you may have 30 or 40 batches in the mail, and several to the same company, put a *sequence* number on the card also. This sequence number will be the number of batches you have out. If this is the 30th batch you have in the mails, put the number 30 on the card. Secure the card with a rubber band to the batch of file cards and file the whole thing in sequence after the last batch under the general title of *Submitted*.

Now put the sequence number somewhere on the back of your return envelope. When your envelope comes back, you will be able to match it quickly with the proper batch of file cards, which will keep you, perhaps, from having to paw through the whole mess to match up some of the returned ideas to file cards.

Another way you can keep track of submitted batches is to keep your file copies in separate files for each company, which is a method a number of writers use. But I believe simply filing them in sequence with a location, or sequence, number is the simplest and quickest method there is.

Sending Queries about Ideas That Have Been Out Too Long. If a batch has been out more than six weeks without any word from the editor, then send a polite query, enclosing a stamped, self-addressed envelope, asking him to check on the status of your ideas. This will ordinarily bring a prompt reply. If you still do not hear within another two weeks, send another query, again enclosing the self-addressed, stamped envelope, and mentioning that this is the second query. If you still do not get an answer; and, unfortunately, there occasionally is an editor who ignores, or is ignorant of, even the basic courtesies to writers; then send the editor a letter stating that if you don't hear from him within 10 days, your ideas (list them) are no longer for sale to his company.

Some writers always register this type of letter and request a return receipt. In any case, always keep a copy of your letter and of the ideas you had submitted for future reference.

If you haven't received an answer from the editor by the end of two weeks, (Allow a few extra days for good measure.) make up new roughs and start submitting them to other companies. I'd also suggest you scratch that particular company off your submission list for a few months. Maybe it will shape up. If and when you do try them again, don't make it good stuff. See how they handle it before you send them anything worthwhile.

What To Do About Batches that Come Back with Ideas Missing. There are a few editors who at times hold ideas out of a batch without mentioning it. Or it sometimes happens that the editor simply forgets to do so. For that reason, *always* count the number of ideas in any returning batch *immediately!* before they have a chance to get mixed up with anything else.

If the editor who has held the ideas decides to buy them, he will either send you a check or a letter/invoice telling you he is buying your ideas. You simply sign the invoice that is at the bottom of the letter and return it to him. Soon after, you receive your check in the mail. (If you *don't* receive your check within thirty days after an editor tells you he is buying something, or you return the invoice, send a polite query about it. Thirty days is long enough to wait.) If he is not going to buy your ideas, he will, of course, return them to you.

There might be times when an editor will write to you and say that he is buying your idea number so and so for so much money (he'll give a rate) and ask you to send him an invoice for the idea. If this happens, you can buy a pad of invoices (statements) at most department and stationery stores. All you do then is type out the editor's name and company at the top of the invoice, put down the code number of the idea and the idea itself, list the price the editor gave you, sign it, and send it in to him. He'll send you a check.

Now, besides the editor holding ideas from your batch, it is also possible, of course, that your ideas have been lost or misplaced. So if ideas are missing and you don't hear anything about them within four to six weeks, a polite query is certainly in order.

Under any condition, the best rule to follow with editors is: When you are in doubt about something, *ask!* Time permitting, you will usually get an answer of some kind. If an editor answers and says he doesn't have your ideas, don't argue with him. He has no reason to lie to you. Keeping your ideas doesn't put money into his pocket. Just make up new roughs and start submitting them again.

If You've Run out of Companies and Your Idea Hasn't Sold. If this happens to you — and if it doesn't, you're a better writer than most — *don't* throw the idea away. Put it away in your file; and then about a year from the date you sent it to the first company on your list, start it circulating again. You may even find before you start recirculating it that you can now see how to improve it, because you will obviously have improved yourself during this time. Above all, *never, never, never give up on any idea as long as you believe it is a good idea!* Always keep your ideas going, revising and updating when you can . . . and remember, *it may sell on its next time out!*

Filing Seasonal Ideas and Ideas that Haven't Sold.   The most straight-forward method of filing, and the one that always proved easiest for me, is to file the ideas under general categories of *birthday, get well, friendship, anniversary, Christmas, Thanksgiving, Easter,* and all the other seasonal days. Some writers break their files down further into captions like *Wife birthday, male get well, better half anniversary,* and so on. I tried this method once, but I found I was spending more time separating and sorting and filing ideas in all those captions than I was doing anything else. I find it quicker to paw through the *birthday* or *get well* or *whathaveyou* category to find a bunch of ideas I want than to try to separate everything into nice little files of their own.

Try the simpler method of filing ideas by categories first and see how it works for you. Then if you feel like you want to break the ideas down further into captions, go to Chapter XII and you'll find most of the commonly used captions listed there for you. Set your files up using those captions, and that is the furthest you should ever want to break your files down. Unless you want to get foolish about it and do nothing but play with your files all the time.

What To Do If You Find a Published Card Identical with an Idea You've Just Sold. The best thing to do is to write the editor who bought your idea and tell him exactly what has happened. If you have not yet been paid for your idea, he will probably stop payment. If the check is on the way to you, return it when you receive it. If you've already received the check and cashed it, the simplest thing, from a bookkeeping standpoint, is for you to replace the idea with the next one the editor picks to buy. This is usually what is done. The editor discards, or returns, the identical idea, and then gets a *free* one from you, his choice, of course. If some time has passed and your idea has been published before you spot the identical card, there is obviously nothing that can be done about it, and so there is no reason to mention it to the editor, but this is another good reason to study the markets constantly.

Remember, part of an editor's job is to constantly study cards on the markets, and it sometimes happens that he spots a card that he has just purchased from a writer. This duplication can happen through pure accident, of course, and it frequently does . . . but if it happens too often to the same writer, the editor will become leery of that writer's work. Make certain that writer isn't you by reading and researching published cards constantly everywhere you can.

Releases. Some editors still write to writers and ask them for a *release* for certain of their ideas that the editor wants to buy. The *release* they are asking for is the same thing that appears on the back of most payment checks for ideas. It is simply a statement that your idea is original, that it has never been sold to anyone else, and that you release all rights to the idea upon payment of the check. To send the editor the release, simply type a statement to that effect, sign it, and send it to him. He'll send you a check.

Income, Expenses and Taxes. After a company has purchased a certain number of ideas from you, it will either ask you for your social security number or will assign a free-lance writer's number to you. At the end of the year it will send you a tax form and also report having paid you x-number of dollars to the infernal bureau of taxes. When you start selling like crazy all those fabulous ideas of yours, it would probably behoove you, somewhere along the line, to have a tax expert advise you on what to report, what expenses to keep track of, what taxes you will have to pay, and, most importantly for you, all those nice things you can deduct. Point: Don't wait until January to do it!

Contributors

Agnes: Conceived in the wispy morning fog under a weeping willow tree, born on the wings of a butterfly held tenderly in the hands of the cool North wind, raised on a mountain side coated with golden leaves of maple and scented needles of pine, fed healthy and strong by the apple-sweet taste of mountain air, shaped into essence by crystal mountain streams, made tall and straight by towering oaks that hold earth and heaven apart, smoothed into beauty by clouds caressing by on scented summer nights, filled with pure clean joy by bubbling mountain springs, infused with tenderness by the creatures who fill the mountain sounds with innocence, and made whole and real by the believing hearts of aging dreams.

Florence Bradley: While she was taking a correspondence course in fiction writing, Florence Bradley's instructor suggested she subscribe to *Writer's Digest.* She did. In it she found a market list of greeting card companies, and so she started writing greeting cards. Although not an instant success, Florence kept at it. As a result, she has sold several hundred greeting cards during the past few years, almost half of them juvenile cards. She has six children who give her juvenile card ideas, and upon whom she tests all her ideas before she sends them out. Recently, she won first place in Juvenile Writing at the Philadelphia Writers Conference, and 2nd place in Article Writing with a piece about studio cards. She presently is a feature writer for *The Atlantic City Press* (New Jersey), does a juvenile column for the *Egg Harbor News,* and also writes and sells light verse and jokes. She has two goals: 1. To write a book that wins the Best Juvenile Book of the Year Award; 2. To become a television comedy writer.

Helen Farries: Editor at Buzza-Cardozo for more than 29 years, Helen is still fascinated with greeting cards as she was when she was a free-lance writer. "No day has ever been long enough for all I wanted to accomplish. I love greeting cards and love what I'm doing. It was my 'dream' to become the editor here when I was free lancing — and that dream came true." In addition to her greeting card work, Helen has collaborated on over seventy ballads, children's songs, and inspirational and sacred music; she writes the lyrics and a friend writes the music. They have an album of inspirational music, and one of their songs was recorded by Mahalia Jackson in her inspiring album, *Mahalia.* Besides being a member of the Soroptimist club for professional women, Helen is also a member of the National Writer's Club, and of ASCAP.

Chris FitzGerald: Chris works both sides of the greeting card street, writing humor and sentiment with equal success. He has written and sold hundreds of greeting cards of every type. Kept busy by the demands of a large family — one wife, nine children, and one abused cat — Chris believes in writing versatility as a means of tapping *all* the markets in the greeting card field, and of maintaining sales during individual editors' slow buying periods. Chris became a full-time free-lance writer in 1966 after serving a seven-year "apprenticeship" in the industry, first as Editorial Supervisor at American Greetings, and then Executive Editorial Director at Gibson Greeting Cards. An English major at Loyola University in Chicago, Chris was editor of the Loyola weekly paper. Since that time he has also worked in the business publication field.

Bob Hammerquist: Native of Brockton, Massachusetts, tentative site for the world's first nuclear powered discount mart. Free-lance gag writer, cartoonist, and successful neighborhood-ne'er-do well. Connoisseur of domestic beers, and semi-professional Scotch quaffer. Journeyman cynic. Docile militant. Three-martini-liberal. Upholder of the Donald Duck ethic. Devastating critic of the immaterial. Honorary Chairman of the Bulgarian Friends of the D.A.R. Currently researching his next literary illusion; an already lightly dismissed probe of the American religious conscience, entitled: "Church Franchises for Profit and Prophet *or* How to Have Your Wafer and Eat it Too."

(Eds. note: Bob wrote the above for himself, but he forgot to mention that he is also one of the top studio card writers in the country . . . and he's not bad in the city, either.)

Ray Mathews: Currently teamed with Jack E. Schneider on an exclusive free-lance contract to provide humorous material to the Paula Greeting Card Company, Ray Mathews has been in the greeting card field since 1952 when he joined the editorial staff of American Greetings. While with that company, he worked in every type of greeting cards, and was their Humorous Editor during his last five years. He has been a full-time free-lance writer since 1963. His contract to provide humorous material to Paula allows him to free lance other types of greeting card material to other companies and so, even though his humor writing demands most of his time and concentration, he still manages to write a fair amount of conventional and inspirational verse. Ray is an Editorial Associate of *Writer's Digest* and, in addition to all his other talents, is also an accomplished composer and lyric writer.

Jack E. Schneider: The other half of the Schneider-Mathews team, Jack began his greeting card career in 1961 when he joined Gibson Greeting

Cards as a color-separation artist after his graduation from the Art Academy of Cincinnati. A year after joining Gibson, he was made Art Director and Editor of their studio card line. In 1963 he moved to the Barker Greeting Card Company to become Chief Editor. A year later he joined the C. M. Paula Company as Creative Director. He left Paul in 1965 with a free-lance contract as designer and gag writer. Soon after, he teamed with Ray Mathews. Besides his greeting card writing and design work, Jack also does cartooning, and has several juvenile books in progress. He is also an Editorial Associate for *Writer's Digest.*

George F. Stanley, Jr.: George F. Stanley, Jr., founded Vagabond Creations in 1957. At that time he published only studio cards, but has since added framed prints, humorous stationery, mottos, and buttons to his outstanding line. Prior to his founding Vagabond, George spent several years with Stanley Greetings, a conventional greeting card publisher. In his role as owner and publisher of Vagabond Creations, George also supervises all editorial and art functions and works in close association with both artists and free-lance writers.

Johnnie Wolfe: After graduating from art school, Johnnie Wolfe joined Gibson Greeting Cards as a Humorous designer. Two years later he became Humorous Editor, and then a few months later Studio-Humorous Editor. In 1963, he left Gibson to become Chief Editor at Barker Greeting Cards. He left Barker in 1964 and has free-lanced ever since. Besides writing studio cards, he also writes humorous card verse, designs cards, and does cartoons. Contrary to Communist inspired rumors, he does not write religious verse. On weekends, he performs at an ultra-plush supper club wowing the overflow crowds by singing in his own inimitable style, playing guitar, emceeing, telling bawdy stories, humoring drunks, balling the women, and generally messing around.

Bibliography

Evans, Bergen and Cornelia Evans, *A Dictionary of Contemporary American Usage,* Randon House, 457 Madison Avenue, New York, N.Y. 10022.

   This is one of the most useful dictionaries there is on word preference, style, grammar, punctuation, and just plain common sense in the use of words. It's a great book, easy to read, easy to understand, and the kind I refer to daily. I write easier and better with it than I could without it. It costs $6.95 and you can buy it from *Writer's Digest* magazine.

Bartlett's Familiar Quotations, Little, Brown and Company, 34 Beacon Street, Boston, Mass. 02106.

   This fantastic collection of old and new quotations becomes more useful and valuable with each edition and revision, and the current one is the biggest and best ever published. There have to be thousands of ideas for conventional and inspirational verses in this book, as well as hundreds of ideas that could be switched into studio cards. Any *one* of those ideas could pay you more than the $15.00 the book now costs. You can buy it from *Writer's Digest* magazine.

The Holy Bible

   The world's greatest source of material for inspirational verses, and also for conventional verses. Using this one book alone, you will never run out of ideas for either type of verses.

Wentworth and Flexner, *Dictionary of American Slang,* Thomas Y. Crowell Company, 201 Park Avenue South, New York, N.Y. 10003.

   This book contains virtually all the slang words and expressions that people presently use. It is an invaluable book to the studio card writer who is often dependent upon the meaning and usage of a particular slang word. Buy it! The $7.50 it costs could easily come back to you in a $50 sale for a gag in which you used a slang word the *right* way. *Writer's Digest* magazine sells it. Buy it there! (This book makes a great and unusual Christmas or birthday present for anyone who is even remotely interested in the way people talk, and it's an even greater present for those *hip* friends of yours.)

Golden Book Dictionaries, Golden Press, Inc., 850 Third Avenue, New York, N.Y. 10022.

   See Chapter VIII about these books. Florence Bradley thinks they're great for getting ideas for juvenile cards. And you can't get a better recommendation than that.

Hardt, Lorraine, *How to Make Money Writing Greeting Cards,* Frederick Fell, Inc., 386 Park Avenue South, New York, N.Y. 10016.

Lorraine Hardt once told me they were giving her book away for free but charging $4.95 for her picture on the cover. That about sets the tone of her book: it's *fun* to read! . . . and it has a lot of good things in it! Two reasons enough for buying it. Besides, as a greeting card writer you should obviously buy all the good books you can on writing greeting cards. This is one of them.

Sutphen, Dick, *Old Engravings and Illustrations,* The Dick Sutphen Studio, Inc., Box 8408, Minneapolis, Minn. 55426.

This book is only one of a series of books that contain *copyright free* (meaning anyone can use them for any purpose free of charge) engravings and illustrations. The books are great for illustrating humorous and studio card gags. Most of the books in the series cost $10, but some of them are less. Mr. Sutphen has a brochure describing the books. Send for it.

Orben, Robert, *Orben's Current Comedy Volumes,* Orben Publications, 3536 Daniel Crescent, Baldwin Harbor, N. Y.

Every month, Mr. Orben publishes a collection of new and topical gags for comedians, disk jockeys, politicians, and whathaveyous. These are sold on a yearly subscription rate. In about November of each year, he gathers up the extra copies of the monthly collections and puts them into a volume, which he then sells at a highly reduced rate. Much of the topical humor is of no value directly because it is now over a year old, but the rest of the volume is priceless for humorous and studio card writers. (Although the topical humor is not of direct value, it is of great use in that it shows all the various ways that topical humor can be written.) Mr. Orben puts out a brochure telling about these volumes and the many other humor books he has written and published. Send for it.

Diller, Phyllis, *Phyllis Diller's Housekeeping Hints,* Doubleday & Company, Inc., 277 Park Avenue, New York, N.Y. 10017.

I love this book for the pure zaniness of it. It's keyed off a lot of ideas for me for anniversary, wedding, and birthday gags. It should do the same for you. But even if it doesn't, it's worth reading for the pure pleasure of it and worth studying for the great examples of how much humor can be packed into a few words. It's also out in paperback — a Fawcett Crest Book.

Roget's International Thesaurus

If you use words, and don't want to use the same ones all the time, you need this book. It's as simple as that. Buy it from *Writer's Digest.* They have it. $2.95 plain, $6.95 thumb-indexed.

Goeller, Carl, *Selling Poetry, Verse and Prose, The Writer,* Inc., 8 Arlington Street, Boston, Mass. 02116.

Carl Goeller is about the most knowledgeable person in the area of creating greeting cards. He put all of his knowledge into a book, called it: *Selling Poetry, Verse and Prose.* Buy it! For $3.95 you can get it from *The Writer* or from *Writer's Digest.*

Gottlieb, Al, *The Gag Recap,* Gag Recap Publications, P.O. Box 86, East Meadow, N.Y. 11554.

This is a recap of published cartoons in all the major magazines. Great material for keying and switching humorous and studio card ideas. You can subscribe to it (it's published monthly) for anywhere from six months (about $7.50) to three years (about $40). Write to Mr. Gottlieb. He'll tell you about it.

The Writer, The Writer, Inc., 8 Arlington Street, Boston, Mass. 02116.

A writer who doesn't subscribe to a writer's magazine has got to be a little weird. Don't be! It's $6.00 a year. Runs a lot of good articles on greeting cards and light verse. Also up-to-date market lists.

Safian, Louis A., *2000 Insults for all Occasions,* The Citadel Press, 222 Park Avenue South, New York, N.Y. 10003.

This book, plus a companion book: *2000 More Insults for all Occasions,* is a fantastic source of humorous and studio card ideas. How do you get them from a book of *insults?* You *reverse* the insult, turn it into a *compliment.* The two books are also out in paperback: Pocket Books.

Webster's New Collegiate Dictionary, G. & C. Merriam Company, Springfield, Mass.

Besides being a good dictionary, this particular book is useful to the greeting card writer because it has a good section on rhyming words in the back.

Webster's New World Dictionary of the American Language (College edition), The World Publishing Company, 119 West 57th Street, New York, N.Y. 10019.

Larger in scope than the Collegiate Dictionary this doesn't have the rhyming words section in it. I'm particularly fond of it, though, because it gives all the different ways that a word can be spelled, including the plural, the -ing, and -ed endings, and all the rest. And I'm nowhere (look it up in your slang dictionary) when it comes to spelling. You can buy this dictionary from *Writer's Digest* for $5.95.

Writer's Digest, F. &. W. Publishing Corporation, 22 East 12th Street, Cincinnati, Ohio 45210.

This book that you are now reading, in which we told you all those great things that will make you a fortune, is published by *Writer's Digest.* If you don't subscribe to *Writer's Digest* magazine ($4.00 a year), don't talk to us! In fact, don't even read our book. You don't deserve it.

Barr, June, *Writing and Selling Greeting Card Verse, The Writer,* Inc., 8 Arlington Street, Boston, Mass. 02116.

If you write greeting cards, you'll want this book. It has many good things in it, any one of which could key off many ideas for you. Buy it! $2.95 from either *The Writer* or *Writer's Digest.*

Armour, Richard, *Writing Light Verse, The Writer,* Inc., 8 Arlington Street, Boston, Mass. 02116.

If you're really serious about being funny in verse, get this book. It tells you more about how to write light, humorous verse than anything else on the market. From *The Writer* or *Writer's Digest* at $3.95.

Also buy the collections of verses put out by greeting card companies such as Buzza-Cardozo, Gibson, Hallmark, and Rust Craft. And try some of the collections of our popular poets like Robert Frost and Carl Sandburg.

For those of you who don't know it, the greeting card industry has its own trade magazine, called, aptly enough, *Greeting Card Magazine.* You can subscribe to it for only $2.00 a year from the Mackay Publishing Co., 95 Madison Ave., N.Y., N.Y. 10016.

Some final thoughts: I always try to get the hardback edition of any reference book I want to keep. I may still be getting ideas from the book 10 years later and a paperback may not last that long. Sometimes I'll buy both the hardback and the paperback editions: the paperback for immediate use, the hardback for keeping.

I haunt used book stores looking for collections of epigrams, jokes, anecdotes, quotations, humorous stories, verses, and anything else I can find that looks like it might be a good source book for ideas. Since it's a used book, it's usually inexpensive, so I can afford to build up a good collection of books that way. In addition, there is always the possibility of my finding an out-of-print collection that no other greeting card writer has. It could turn out to be my own personal gold mine. Or yours, if you get to it first!

Glossary of Greeting Card Terms

Action: The items or processes that produce a movement or effect.

Action Card: A card that contains an action.

Art Director: The person who directs the functions of the Art Department; usually responsible for both staff and free-lance art work.

Artwork: The illustrations and lettering on a greeting card.

Attachment: An object fastened; attached; to a greeting card.

Batch: A group of cards submitted together in one envelope.

Beading: A coating or finish consisting of small glass or plastic beads.

Black and White: The basic card illustration sketched by the artist without color. Looks somewhat like a black and white cartoon.

Body Humor: Humor based upon functions or actions of or upon the body that are outside the realm of sex humor; e.g. Belly button and bedpan gags would be body humor. Body humor is sometimes inappropriately called *toilet humor.*

Buildup: The first part of a gag that sets up the reader for the punchline. Sometimes called lead-in or feed line . . . usually given entirely on the cover of a card.

Caption: Ordinarily, the specific purpose or individual for which the card is intended. For example: Mother — Mother's Day, Female — Birthday, Girl — Graduation. May at times designate individual or group sending card. For example: Mother's Day — From Daughter, Get Well — From Group.

Card Code: A numerical or alphabetical group assigned to a specific verse or gag as a means of rapid identification.

Category: A broad grouping or classification used to designate cards for similar occasions. For example: Birthday, Anniversary, Get Well, and Friendship are all separate categories.

Color Separation: 1. A photographic process in which colors are separated or isolated through the use of color filters. 2. A mechanical process in which the artist opaques (blacks) in on a sheet of acetate (a clear plastic material) the area where a color is desired. This is done for each color on the card. When sent to the engraver, the opaqued areas become solid raised areas on the printing plate. Ink of the desired color is then used to coat the raised areas. The ink is transferred to the paper by pressure, the operation is repeated for each color. The printing process is similar to that employed when you use a rubber hand-stamp.

Contemporary: 1. Studio. 2. Belonging to the present time.

Conventional: 1. General. 2. Formal or sentimental cards, usually done in verse or simple one line prose.

Cover: The front outside of a card, sometimes called *page one.*

Creative Director: Person in charge of Creative Department, which usually consists of Art Department and Editorial Department. Creative Director is often, but not necessarily, a Vice President of the company.

Cutes: 1. Soft humored, slightly sweet feminine-type cards in which the text is closely tied to the illustration. Physically, may be of varying sizes. 2. Informals.

Design: The whole layout of a greeting card, including illustrations, type of lettering, color, and placement of all of these on the card.

Die Cut: Cutting a card into some other than its normal shape; e.g. in the shape of an animal illustrated on the cover.

Dummy: A form shaped like a greeting card with a rough illustration and lettering, used to submit ideas.

Editor: Person in charge of Editorial Department and/or responsible for all the ideas in a particular line, such as studio line; may also write a portion of the line.

Editor-In-Chief: Head of Editorial Department that consists of several editors and writers.

Engraver: The person who forms the art work impressions upon metal plates in preparation for printing.

Everydays: Cards for occasions that occur *every day* of the year, such as birthdays and anniversaries.

Finish: 1. A completed card design, including final artwork, color separation, and lettering. 2. Material used on the cover of a card — e.g. flocking or beading.

Flocking: A material having a felt-like feel and appearance, used as a finish on a card.

French Fold: A method of folding often used for humorous and conventional cards. Basic fold consists of using a sheet of paper four times the final size of the card, then folding the paper down in half once, and then folding the resultant sheet across in half once. Also used for multi-page cards. Purpose of fold is so that all printing can be done on one side of the paper only. A less expensive method when color is used on inside illustrations as is often done on conventional and humorous cards.

General: See conventional.

Holds: Denotes the ideas an editor retains for further consideration or for a product or line planning meeting.

Humor Formula: A loosely set category for designating a type of joke or gag.

Humorous: A card in which the sentiment is expressed humorously. Text may be in either verse or prose, but is normally in verse. The illustration is usually tied closely to the text, and much of the humor is derived from the illustration itself. Published in various sizes. Often illustrated with animals.

Idea: Used synonymously with *verse* or *gag,* especially for studio cards.

Idea Bank: A reserve or surplus of ideas that an editor has bought but not yet published.

Informals: See Cutes.

Inside Left: Counting the cover of a normal two-fold card as page 1, the inside left would be page 2, and the back of the card page 4.

Inside Right: Page 3 of a normal two-fold card. See *inside left.*

Invoice: A statement listing the code number of your idea, the idea itself, and the price the editor has offered for it.

Juveniles: Cards designed to be sent to children, usually up to about age 12. Mostly written to be sent *from* adults.

Lead-In: See *buildup.*

Letterer: A person who marks or draws the letters and numbers on a card.

Line: 1. A row of words in a verse. 2. The words on the cover of a studio card, *or* the words on the inside; commonly called *outside line, inside line.* 3. All of the same types or series of cards published by a company, usually broken down roughly into broad groupings — e.g. studio line, humorous line, everyday line, Christmas line, seasonal line, etc. A very general classification.

Local Imprints: Cards that are intended to be sent from a specific city or area. Cards are usually headed with words somewhat like: "Hello from..................." Name of city or area is left out when cards are initially printed. City or area is specially imprinted when cards are ordered.

Market Letter: The list of categories and themes of ideas an editor needs. Some companies publish market letters on a regular basis, others only when the need arises.

Mechanical: Pertains to a card that contains an action of some type.

Needs: Types of ideas an editor requires, or *needs.*

Neuter: A character depicting neither sex; could be either male or female.

Novelty: Refers to ideas that fall outside the realm of greeting cards, although they may be sent for the same occasion as greeting cards, and that may be boxed differently and sold at different prices from standard greeting card prices.

Pop-Up: A mechanical action in which a form protrudes from the inside of the card when the card is opened.

Premise: The basic idea around which a gag or verse is built. In the gag: "Wanted to smuggle some of my homemade brew in to you to help you feel better . . . but it ate right through your enema bag!" the premise is: *smuggling homemade brew in to a patient in a hospital.*

Promotions: Usually a series or group of cards (although promotions are not confined to cards) that have a common feature and are given special sales promotion.

Prose: The ordinary language used in speaking and writing, as opposed to verse and poetry.

Punchline: That last part of a gag or joke in which the denouement is contained.

Punch-Outs: Sections of a card, usually Juvenile, that are perforated so that they can be easily removed.

Rates: The amount that an editor pays for each line of verse or for an idea totally.

Reader: The person reading the card.

Receiver: The person who receives the card.

Recipient: See Receiver.

Rejects: The ideas or verses that have not been bought by the editor and are returned.

Rejection Slip: Ecccct-ky thing!

Requirements: See *needs.*

Return Envelope: A stamped, self-addressed envelope that you include with the batch or request you submit so that the editor can return rejected ideas or requested material to you.

Risque: Ideas that joke about sex.

SASE: Self-addressed, Stamped Envelope.

Seasonals: Cards published for the several special days that we observe during the year — e.g. Christmas, Graduation, Halloween, etc.

Sendability: Pertains to the degree to which a particular idea or card is appropriate for a specific occasion and for the largest possible number of senders and receivers.

Sender: The person who sends the card.

Series: A limited number of cards in which something common, such as theme, action, attachment, or finish, has been used.

Sex Humor: Humor based upon male/female sex relations.

Slam: Insulting humor.

Spinner: A device that spins. Usually is in the shape of an arrow or is pointed at one end.

Staff-Writer: A writer who works full time for a company, on company premises, and is paid a salary.

Statement: See *invoice.*

Studio: 1. Contemporary. 2. Cards that use short, punchy gags that are in keeping with current humor vogues and trends. Always rectangular in shape.

Suggestive Humor: Sex humor or body humor.

Tag Line: The line or words that designate the occasion and transmit the wish or basic sentiment. For example: Happy Birthday, Get Well Soon, Merry Christmas, Happy New Year. The tag line is usually either the first line or the last line on a card.

Themes: The subject or topic of a verse or gag. For example: love, drinking, sex, compliment, etc.

Three-Fold: A card, usually studio, that is folded twice, just as you would fold a business letter. The last fold, or section, may be folded inward to the center of the card, or outward to the back of the card.

Timely: Ideas or cards containing subjects that are seasonably or opportunely timed. Sometimes used to mean *topical,* but should not be: ideas using Tiny Tim as a subject would be *timely* for Christmas, *untimely* for Halloween, and *topical* for neither.

Toilet Humor: See *body humor.*

Topical: Ideas or cards containing subjects that are currently the topic of discussion. Sometimes used in the same sense as *timely,* but should not be. A subject may be timely because of the season (e.g. witches at Halloween), but not be of sufficient interest to be a general topic of discussion.

Vari-Vue: Trade name for flat, glass-like devices that appear to contain moving illustrations. For example, female lips that are either pursed or smiling depending on the angle at which you view the device. Also have such illustrations as bucking horses, flying witches, vibrating hearts, and winking eyes.

Verse: Usually refers to a line of poetry that has a metrical or rhythmical pattern, but at times used to mean any text on a card. Thus, a studio card gag written in prose might be referred to as a verse; incorrectly so, of course.

Virko: A shellac type finish used on cards.

Wish: 1. To express a desire that someone have happiness, good fortune, good will, or good health. 2. To express a desire or yearning for someone or something.

Index